Dottie —
hope there are
a few recipes in here
that bring your family
great enjoyment

Karen Calarco

Josie's Recipe Collection:

From Cooks and Kitchens of Central New York

Edited by
Karen M. Talarico

authorHOUSE

1663 Liberty Drive, Suite 200
Bloomington, Indiana 47403
(800) 839-8640
www.authorhouse.com

First published by AuthorHouse 08/04/04

ISBN: 1-4184-6867-3 (e)
ISBN: 1-4184-6865-7 (sc)
ISBN: 1-4184-6866-5 (dj)

Printed in the United States of America
Bloomington, Indiana

This book is printed on acid-free paper.

Table of Contents

DRINKS, SNACKS and RELISHES   20

COOKIES 40

ENTREES 87

Josephine Marie Talarico

Born on July 5, 1914 in her childhood home at 216 Fourth Avenue in Frankfort, New York, Josie was the oldest of six children of Lucy and Guiseppe Sgroi and her father's namesake. She attended local schools and graduated from Frankfort High School in 1930.

She married in 1944 at the then St. Mary's Catholic Church in Frankfort and became Josephine Talarico. The mother of four children: Richard, Karen, Lucy and Sam, the family resided at 696 Second Ave Extension in Frankfort. Her life was making a home, raising her children and cooking and baking. Her recipe collection was vast. This volume represents only 60% of her recipes. There are over 300 recipes in this book. She had a simple philosophy, "If you can read, you can bake."

She lived the last 15 years of her life at the Mid-Town Apartments in Herkimer, New York on Prospect Street. While living there she made a great many new friendships. More recipes to exchange! Josephine passed away on March 29, 2002.

The Frankfort Girls that married after World War II, grew up together and grew old together, made lasting friendships and are the soul of this collection. Family recipes from Utica, New York are also included. Her husband's family lived on Leeds Street in Utica.

The recipes that were selected for this book are old family favorites and were frequently made by either Josephine or other great family cooks. They are representative of Italian life for holidays, everyday meals, Sunday specials and family events. Josie's friendships formulated the basis for this book. Friendship was their recipe for life.

One of the old family favorites, became an after school treat, which were sold at the family's gas station. Daily she would bake fancy cupcakes, cream filled or piled high with homemade frosting, to the delight of many Frankfort students.

When it was time for weddings, showers, graduations and other family occasions, her sister Mary would arrive late at night just in time to watch Johnny Carson and bake cookies. They would spend all night baking hundreds of cookies for trays.

Josephine's dream was to have a winning recipe for the annual Pillsbury Bakeoff Contest. In 1958 the Pillsbury Bakeoff Contest came to New York. Josie entered but did not win. She came home with only a consolation cookbook.

However in the early 1960's, Josie was chosen by the local baker to be his assistant. At that time, Latella's Bakery was located on Main Street in Frankfort and the owner delivered bread to the family home. While making his daily rounds, he would see the array of baked goods that Josie set out on the front porch to cool. He was so pleased by her talent that she worked for him for three years until he sold his business.

When Josie came home with only that consolation cookbook from the Pillsbury Bakeoff Contest, little did she know her life would become a cookbook in the making.

DEDICATION

For all the wonderful women who made this collection possible, this compilation is proof of their existence and how their friendship touched Josie's life…this is a testimonial to all of their lives, their work and the love they unselfishly gave to their families. The art of their lives lies within these pages. It was such a joy to read every word and live each recipe. Happy reading…and happy eating to all those who enter this volume!

The children of Josie Sgroi Talarico

The Story

It all began at 216 Fourth Ave, the home of my maternal grandparents. My grandfather came from Italy when he was just 17 years old, arriving through Ellis Island. He married my grandmother Lucy. My mother is the oldest of four girls and two boys. My mother's youngest brother was killed in an accident when he was just a little boy.

Mother was born in 1914 and married in 1944. I am Karen her oldest daughter, the inheritor and editor of this lovely cookbook. The recipes she collected are a journey and testimonial of my mother's life of the friends she made along the way and with whom she shared her life.

Her sister Mary was her soul mate and other self. Sometimes it was difficult to tell them apart. Julia, a much younger sister was not much of a culinary arts person herself, unlike Mary and my mother who inherited their mother's panache in the kitchen. But Julia was an artist and her splendid paintings were her contribution to the legacy of the sisterhood.

For some reason there are no recipes from her sister Dorothy the baby sister. But Grandma Lucy would love knowing that Aunt Dot's grandsons currently make and sell great pizza in the Mohawk Valley, even if it is not an old family recipe. Oddly enough there are no family recipes in here for pizza (Aunt Mary's was the best) or Grandma's thick tomato pie. These were everyday recipes that they made from scratch and didn't need to write down.

There were neighbors of my grandmother who lived on Fourth Ave, Mrs. Harvey and Alta Coombs who have recipes as part of this collection. As well as my sister Lucy, who is her grandma's name-sake. Vicki is the wife of my oldest brother. A recipe from Lena's kitchen appears. She was married to my mother's brother.

My father's sister Angie was a marvelous cook and baker; a few of her masterpieces are a part of this collection. She appears as Angie, Aunt Angie and Angie Sassone, one in the same. Antoinette and Rita were married to my father's brothers. Nana is my paternal grandmother.

When I was 8 or 9 years old, my mother went to driving school; there was no stopping her now. She was out and about in the neighborhood. She took sewing lessons. She loved to read and collect recipes. "I like food", she'd say.

When her children were older, my mother worked as a cook in the school cafeteria. She was also a housekeeper for the Bennison's, both the father the elder Mr. Bennison and Mr. Bennison's son and family.

Mary Lore (Cross is her married name) was her school friend and life long friend. They died within days of each other in 2002. Her girlfriends, cousins and indeed second cousins-there was Carm Bono, Pauline and Julia Frank, Mary Carboni, Mary Valent, Mary Sylvester, Mamie Oriole and Josie and Rose Barberio, they were friends and shared a special sisterhood. This book is a tribute to their lives. These women and homemakers of the 1940's-60's who raised baby boomer children. They were stay at home moms that made life pour out of their kitchens.

This is not a beginner's cookbook. The cook needs to be able to visualize the finished product and jump right into the recipe like a dancer in a chorus line. These women were artists and they created a life with food for special occasions, holidays and everyday dinners.

Special Acknowledgement: Editors Note

The "rebirth" of this edition of recipes would not likely have come about without the urgings of my daughter Kimmy Ann. This cookbook for years existed as two tattered three-ring volumes on the bottom shelf of a cabinet in my mother's living room. Kim saw it as a tribute to her Grandmother's life.

Many years ago my mother started to place pieces of masking tape on items in her household that she wanted family and friends to inherit. This practice became somewhat of a joke. After returning from studying in Italy my daughter said to me have Grandma put a piece of tape on her cookbooks for you. She felt that the food she ate in Italy in the small towns was much like the food she was raised on as a young girl in New York. My daughter felt that the recipes needed to be handed down to the next generation.

Her grandmother was so thrilled that Kim actually got to travel to Italy, a dream she herself was never able to fulfill. Kim sent her Grammie, as she on rare occasion would affectionately speak of her, a postcard from Italy that my mother cherished. I found that postcard in my mother's papers that she kept on a little table by her chair when I cleaned her apartment after she passed away.

So, at Kim's insistence I called my mother one day some years back and half jokingly said "Ma, put a piece of tape on the cookbooks for me!" Nothing more was ever said I just assumed that I would someday take the books home with me. After she died and I was sorting her belongings, sure enough on the cookbooks was a tattered piece of tape with "Karen" written on it.

My daughter is **my** other self. She loved her Grandmother very much. I usually called my mother "Josie". I had often called my daughter "Josie" as they were a lot alike. When I returned from New York and my mother's funeral, I looked through the books one night with my daughter on the telephone. We had laughs at some of the writings and gasped at recipes I hadn't come across in years. I decided that evening that I would retype it and pass it on. Something I always intended to do. But that night I realized that this book was the true testimonial to her life, and her existence both as a mother and as a woman. Thanks to my sister Lucy who found a few recipes and helped to put a face to some names I couldn't remember.

I have tried to edit both volumes with Josie's life in mind. Some recipes bring back memories. I tried to make notations that brought the recipes to life. I felt the notes she made in the margins were like hearing from her again, little letters to herself that allowed us to hear her voice again.

The recipes are, as I found them, with their omissions and free-style in their creativity. As I said this is not a beginner's cookbook. Jump in and enjoy! So thanks to my mother and my daughter for a sisterhood of laughs and good times. I hope everyone enjoys this book and cherishes the labor of love that Josie created for us all. The actual two tattered volumes I am giving to my daughter for her to cherish.

BREADS

Grandma Lucy   July 1961

Josie's Recipe Collection:

Egg Bread

(very good) makes 3 loaves

1½ cup scalded milk
½ cup Crisco
4½ tbsps sugar
3 eggs beaten
2 tsps salt
1½ cups cool water
2 pkgs yeast
10 cups flour
For cinnamon loaf I doubled sugar and cut salt in half

That's it! that's the recipe...you have to know how to make bread or you are out of luck!...shaping, pan size, oven temperature...have at it

Basic Dough for Pizza

3-3 ½ cups flour
1 pkg dry yeast
1½ tsps salt
1 cup hot water
½ tsp sugar
1 tbsp oil
makes 2 12" or 14" pizzas or 1 stuffed pizza

she refers to this Basic dough in other recipes

Pumpkin Bread (Lucy's)

3 c sugar
1 can-16 oz pumpkin
1 c oil
3 ½ c flour
4 eggs beaten
3 tsps soda
2 tsps salt
1 tsp b. powder
1 tsp nutmeg-1 tsp all spice-1 tsp cinnamon-½ tsp cloves
⅔ cup water
1 cup nuts-1 cup raisins

cream sugar & oil add eggs and pumpkin- mix well-sift dry
ingredients-add dry in–alternate with water
Pour into well greased & floured 9x5 pans (2)
Bake 350 –1½ hrs-Let stand 10 min before removing form
pans

There were actual dried pumpkin bread batter remnants on this page!

Josie's Recipe Collection:

Calzone (basic dough)

1 # hot & sweet sausage fried & cut in ½" slices
1 T olive oil
After sausage is fried-combine 3 lge peppers cut in strips-
3 med onions sliced-3 lge cloves of garlic minced-1½ tsps salt-
1 tsp oregano-¼ tsp pepper-olive oil

Sauté 10 min-add sausage and 3 Tbsps tomato paste-Let cool

Divide one basic dough recipe in half-Roll 1 piece to 16"x8" rectangle and cut in half length wise and quarter crosswise (8"x4" squares)

Top center of each square with ⅓ cup filling-Bring up 2 opposite corners, overlap slightly-pinch to seal

Transfer to prepared cookie sheet greased and sprinkled with cornmeal. Serve warm or at room temp-Repeat with remaining dough
16 squares-225 calories each

well I can't recall ever having one of these, no cheese?!

Savory Batter for Deep Fat Frying

Heat to 350 degrees

Combine 2 egg yolks-⅓ c milk-⅓ c water-1 Tbsp lemon juice-
1 Tbsp margarine or butter (melted)-1 c sifted flour-½ tsp salt
Fold in 2 stiffly beaten egg whites
Pan must be half full of oil (no more) just to cover food
Replace salt with sugar for sweet fritters

Zucchini Bread

1 cup Crisco

2 cups sugar (try less)
3 eggs
3 tsp vanilla
2 cups grated zucchini
1 cup walnuts (optional)

3 cups flour (minus 3 Tbsps)
1 tsp salt
¼ tsp B. powder
1 tsp B. soda
3 tsp. Cinnamon

grease bread pan or Bundt pan
Bake 350 degrees-55-60 min

In the margin she noted that 1 ½ cups of sugar was "okay" and under Bundt pan she wrote "all but 1 cup batter"

Bread (Carm Bono's)

13 c flour
3 c water
1 c milk
4 tsps salt
1 tsp sugar
1 Tbsp melted Spry
2 pkgs yeast
Let rise 1 hour-Punch down-Let rise 1 hour-knead-shape-Let rise 1 hour. Bake at 375 degrees-45-60 min
Makes 4 loaves-round pie tin
Makes 3 rectangle & 1 round 9" pizza

For Herb Bread

Add 1 pkg dry ranch style buttermilk salad dressing mix-reserve 1 tsp-sprinkle on warmed baked bread after brushing with butter
(for 6 c flour) Substitute 1 ½ c buttermilk for some of the water and 1 egg. Bake 25-30 minutes-375 degrees

I believe this recipe refers to Carm's bread recipe above... and 6 cups will cut this recipe in half

Mary Lazzuri's Easter Bread

	¼ of recipe
14 eggs beaten	3 ½ eggs
3 cups sugar	¾ c sugar
1 lb oleo	¼ lb or 1 stick oleo
3 tsp vanilla	¾ tsp vanilla
2 envelopes of yeast-dissolved in warm milk	1 envelope yeast
2 cups milk	½ cup milk
18 cups flour	4½ cups flour

Let rise once-shape dough let rise again-bake at 325 to 350 degrees, Brush with egg & a little water

Spinach Turnover (Carm Bono)

3 # raw spinach chopped-1 cup raisins **(use more)**-a big tablespoon melted shortening-red pepper-2 pinches of salt-hot pepper-½ clove garlic
Make pastry same as for sausage pies
She noted this: For 10 oz spinach I used 2 big Tbsps of Crisco-1½ pinches of salt-more cloves of garlic-paprika and red pepper flakes-½ recipe for pastry-1 cup raisins-takes longer to bake than the sausage pies

Pizza Stuffed with Broccoli

(use Basic Dough)

1 bunch (1-1¼ #) broccoli cut into small florets-olive oil-½ # mushrooms thickly sliced-3 large garlic cloves (minced)-½ t salt divided-¼ c roasted red peppers cut into ½" pieces-½ t freshly ground pepper

¼ c grated Parmesan cheese	1 cup ricotta cheese
½ # mozzarella shredded	1 egg slightly beaten
½ # provolone cheese cubed	¼ # sliced Genoa salami (halved)

Lightly brush a 12" or 14" pizza pan with olive oil-Sprinkle with cornmeal-set aside-divide dough into 2 pieces-one slightly larger. Roll large piece to fit pan with a ½" overhang <u>Filling:</u> In med. Saucepan cook florets in boiling salted water, two min, Drain-set aside. In med skillet heat 2T olive oil-add mushrooms & garlic-½ tsp salt. Sauté in med heat until golden & liquid has evaporated (about 10 min). Add broccoli-peppers-green pepper & ½ tsp salt. Mix well. Let cook. Have oven rack on lowest position-Preheat oven to 450 degrees (?). Sprinkle Parmesan & mozzarella over dough in pan. Spoon broccoli mixture over cheese to within 1" of edge - Scatter salami & provolone over broccoli- In small bowl combine ricotta & egg-spoon over filling. Roll remaining dough to a 12" or 14" circle. Place over filling-Turn up overhang & pinch to seal-Bake until golden brown-15-20 min-Cool 10 min before cutting
8 slices from pizza each 560 calories
she had these notes: about $6.00 for filling...yeah what year...400 degrees 15 min and 425 degrees 10 min...she must have experimented with different cooking times...at least this recipe has directions

Pastry Dough (Spinach Bread etc.)

8 cups of flour (9½ if sifted)
1 ¾ cups of Crisco
1 ½ tsp salt
2 tsp baking powder
2 ¼ cups cold water

this was not in the cook book but Josie had just given it to Kimmy Ann; hint of the day you can use ready made pie crust...I guess when she turned 80- ish she cut corners...she said Gina (her granddaughter) gave her the idea for ready crust no directions...just mix and go I guess

Pastry for Sausage Pies

8 c flour (9½ c sifted)-¾ # Spry (1¾ c)-1½ tsp salt-2 tsps b. powder-water (about 2¼ c)
Bake large turnovers about 20 min lower shelf and 15 min top-bake small turnovers about 10 min bottom and 10 min top-bake cookie sheets ½ hr-Bake at 375 degrees

Note: makes about 5 large-4 small turnovers; instead of turnovers make cookie sheets

Ricotta Spinach Pie

2 T butter or oleo
¼ c chopped green onions
10 oz pkg frozen spinach (thawed and drained)
15 oz ricotta
½ cup grated Parmesan cheese
4 eggs beaten
⅓ c finely chopped prosciutto
¼ tsp salt
¼ tsp nutmeg

1 egg beaten for glaze
pastry (as above)

In med skillet melt butter, add onions-sauté until translucent, cool slightly; add spinach-cook until all butter is absorbed. In lge bowl combine ricotta-spinach & onions. Add 4 eggs-ham-cheese-salt-pepper & nutmeg. Mix well-Preheat oven to 425 degrees. Brush outer edge with beaten egg. Add filling cover with remaining pastry-place on oven rack on low position. Bake 20 min-Serve warm-6-8 servings.

Found this on the email Kim sent me with the recipe. Bake 10 min. @ 375 degrees; Brush with egg wash, bake another 10 minutes or until golden brown.

Ham Pie (Marie Sanita's)

½ # salami sliced & cut up-1 # ricotta-black pepper & salt to taste-1 stick pepperoni cut up-4 raw eggs-1 thick sliced ham chopped-parsley and a handful of grated cheese-4 hard boiled eggs sliced-Bake 1-1½ hrs at 350 degrees

This is another filling for turnover or cookie sheet pies

Josie's Recipe Collection:

Carrot Bread

2 cups flour	½ cup flaked coconut
2 tsps soda	½ cup chopped pecans
2 tsps cinnamon	1 cup vegetable oil **(try ¾)**
½ tsp salt	2 tsps vanilla
1½ cups sugar	2 cups grated raw carrots
½ cup dried currants	3 eggs

Mix dry ingredients together-add currants-coconut and nuts. Add remaining ingredients & mix well. Pour into 3 greased 1 lb. veg. or fruit cans. Let stand 20 minutes. Bake in mod oven 350 degrees 1 hour. Cool slightly, remove from cans. When cold-wrap and refrigerate
Bread will keep up to 2 weeks in the refrigerator; it can also be frozen

(Mom's note: a little too much for 3 tins, try an extra, <u>small</u> loaf pan)

Brown Bread (Mrs. Williams) my sewing instructor

1 cup sweet milk-1 c sour milk-2 c graham flour-1 c flour-½ c molasses-1 egg-2 tsps b. soda-1 scant tsp b. powder-salt. Bake in mod oven for 45 min. Cover first half hour. This makes 2 small loaves (1 Tbsp of shortening to a loaf may be added)

Pound Loaf (Miva's)

¾ lb. butter-½ tsp salt-1 lb. sugar-8 eggs-4 c flour-½ c sour cream-½ c cornstarch-4 tsp b. powder; about 1½ cups fruits and nuts-chopped fine and floured. Bake in 350 degree oven-1 hr or more. Makes 2 loaves-may be iced-lemon glaze or vanilla

another mix and fix... and who is Miva?

Date Bread (Helen Miller)

1 cup dates stoned (**I guess she means pitted)** & cut fine-
1 c boiling water –pour over dates and let stand until soft-
½ c nut meats cut fine, 1 Tbsp butter or Crisco-scant ½ tsp salt-
¾ c sugar, 1 tsp. b. soda dissolved in ½ c warm water. 1 egg
well beaten-1½ tsps b. powder-2¾ c flour sifted together.

Cream shortening & sugar-stir well-add dates-then soda, then
flour & b. powder-nut meats & vanilla; Line pan with waxed
paper, Bake in loaf pan for 40 min. at 350 degrees-reduce heat
for 10 or 15 min. Let stand overnight to ripen.

**I think I would put the vanilla in when creaming the eggs
and butter; nothing about draining excess water from dates
either...what does that ripen thing mean?**

Bagels

¼ cup oleo-1 cup scalded milk (or water), 1 tsp salt-1 pkg yeast,
½ c sugar-1 or 2 eggs, about 4 c sifted flour-about 1½ tsps anise
or fennel seed
Add oleo, sugar & salt to milk. Cool; to lukewarm and add
yeast-egg & flour. Let rise about 1 hr or until double in bulk.
Punch down & shape & put on greased sheet. Let rise 20 min
or until puffy. Bake about 20 min. or until golden brown.
350-375 degrees. After 10 min. of baking I brushed them with
egg wash
To make Italian bagels omit sugar-just use 1 tsp sugar in
yeast mixture-fennel seeds, use anise seeds in sweet dough or
caraway seeds. If bagels are large bake at 350 degrees.

Sausage Pies (Carm Bono)

4 # sausage-2 c grated cheese-14 eggs. Cook sausage until half
done. Add cheese and eggs
This is a filling for pastry that makes turnovers and alike

Sausage Pies (Angie's)

3 # sausage fried-5 hard boiled eggs-½ # mozzarella-4 or 5 eggs to bind-parsley-blk. pepper-¾ c grated cheese

Notes: in 1997 made 16 7 ½ " pie plate..."bind", yeah right, your coronary arteries!!

Pork Chop Pies

8 pork chops partially cooked & cubed-5 beaten eggs-1½ c grated cheese-parsley-black. pepper-makes 2 turnovers-Bake at 400 degrees

recipe was so old and paper deteriorated that the length of cooking time is obliterated...go ahead give it a try

Tiralli (Carm Bono)

(makes about 70)
5 # flour-1 # Spry (2 c + 6 Tbsp)-2 pkgs yeast, 2 Tbsps+2 tsps
salt-2 Tbsps fennel seed water (about 3¼ c)
Start shaping tiralli immediately after mixing dough. By the
time you finish shaping, the first ones will be ready to bake (if
they look puffy)
Hot oven 400 degrees-Egg yolk glaze, 10 min. on lower shelf-
10 min. on upper shelf,
When making thicker tiralli bake at 375 degrees

⅓ of recipe:

6⅔ c flour
2 eggs
⅔ c + 2 T Spry
1 yeast
2⅔ tsp salt
2 tsp fennel
1 c + 4 tsp water

Old Fashioned Tiralli (Flora Cavaretta)

5 # flour-¾ lb lard melted in 1 quart of water. Cool-pinch of salt-pinch of fennel-3 pkgs yeast. Shape-let rise-Put in boiling water-lift out with perforated ladle-place on greased baking sheet 400 degrees-15min

⅓ recipe:

6⅔ c flour
¼ # lard
1⅓ c water
little salt and fennel seed
1 pkg yeast

water for the dough itself and dissolving yeast...you are on your own

Pepperoni Pies

2 sticks pepperoni-½ # steam ham-¼ # sliced salami-4 hard boiled eggs-½ of a basket of cheese-½ c grated cheese-blk pepper-4 raw eggs

notes: enough to fill a cookie sheet-this is my version of Ham Pie

Crust: 2 c flour-1 egg-¾ c Crisco-salt & pepper to suit-water-rub crust with egg

Brown and Serve White Bread –3 loaves

2 pkgs yeast-4 c warm water-⅜ c sugar-¾ c non fat dry milk-1 Tbsp + 1 tsp salt-⅜ c butter or oleo-melted and cooled-12 to 13 c flour
When bread has doubled in bread pans-Pre-bake in preheated 275 degree oven for 30-35 min.(or until bread begins to color lightly) Wrap-Freeze

To serve-Bake on greased cookie sheet preheated 400 degree oven-30 min. if it gets to brown before time is up cover with foil.

Orange Rolls

1 pkg yeast-¼ c water-1 cup milk scalded-⅓ c sugar-½ c shortening-1 tsp salt-5-5½ c flour-2 beaten eggs-¼ c orange juice-2 Tbsps grated orange rind-see below recipe for glaze
Mix dough as usual-Cover-let rise 10 min.-knead dough 5-10 min. on lightly floured surface until smooth.
Place in lightly greased bowl-turning over to grease surface.
Cover let rise until double in bulk (2 hrs ?)
Punch down & cover-let rest 10 min. Shape.
<u>Bow-knots</u>-strips 10"x¾"-roll lightly make bowknot-arrange on cookie sheet-tucking ends under. Let rise until double-Bake 400 degrees-12 min.

Orange Icing- 1 tsp grated orange peel-1 cup xxxx sugar-2 Tbsps orange juice

I'm confused here; does the rest of the orange juice and rind go into the dough...
She notes if you double the recipe use 12 cups of flour...she checked this and it was OK

15

Easy Carrot Bread (4 mini loaf pans)

1 c oil-1 c sugar-3 eggs-1½ c sifted flour-1½ Tbsps b. soda-1 tsp b. powder-1 tsp cinnamon- 1 tsp allspice-¼ tsp nutmeg-3 cups grated carrots-½ c chopped walnuts or pecans. Grease the mini loaf frame. Preheat oven 325 degrees. In a lge mixing bowl, combine oil-sugar & eggs-beat-stir in flour-b. soda-b. powder-cinnamon-allspice-nutmeg & carrots. Stir until carrots are coated with the batter-Mix in nuts-Spoon batter into the mini loaf pans-filling them almost to the top. Bake in middle of oven until a toothpick comes out clean but moist-about 45 min. Let cool on rack for 10 min-turn the mini loaves out to cool further

Egg Bread (Angie's)

12 eggs-pinch of salt for each egg
1 cup of sugar
½ # margarine
(beat these 3 together)

1 cup warm milk
2 yeast cakes dissolved ¼ cup warm water
peel from 1 orange (grated)
about 12 cups of flour (maybe more)
Make sure dough is soft. Let rise until double in bulk (3-4 hrs)
Shape in braids or whatever way you want. Let rise again for 1 hr.
Bake in 350 degree oven until golden brown (25-30 min)
Spread white of egg on top before baking

These notes on the recipe: she revised the recipe to 1 cup of sugar from 2 cups and 1 cup of milk instead of 2 cups; you can use 1 yeast cake if mixed overnight (11:00 PM –8:00 AM)…yeast cakes! Haven't seen one of those since the 50's! I use fast yeast. I remember that Nana mixed bread before she went to bed at night and in the morning it was ready to bake or make fried dough for breakfast

Overnight Cinnamon Coffee Cake or Buns (Karen's)

4 c flour-1 tsp salt-¼ c sugar-¼ cup butter-¼ cup shortening (Crisco)-¼ c warm water-1pkg yeast-3 egg yolks beaten-1 cup milk scalded and cooled

Put flour, salt and sugar in a bowl-cut in shortening-dissolve yeast in water-add eggs and milk-then add to flour-Beat well.

Chill overnight. In the morning divide dough and roll into two rectangles-brush with melted butter then sprinkle with ¼ c sugar plus ¾ tsp cinnamon. Roll up like a jelly roll and cut into slices. Cover let rise-Bake at 350-375, 20-25 minutes. Brush on glaze.

Makes 2 loaves or 2 doz rolls (maybe baked in muffin pans)

Following marginal notes: used ½ c butter this was used and checked as well as ½ cup of shortening...she quadrupled the fat...yikes! The note says Karen's recipe...but I truly do not remember this...maybe it was a 70's thing when I baked more.

Easter Pie (Mary Carboni's)

1 # of sausage fried	1 # Italian fresh cheese
6 hard boiled eggs	1 # ham
1½ # ricotta	3 or 4 eggs well beaten (six may be used)

Crust: 4 eggs-½ cup milk-pinch of salt-2 Tbsps Spry-2 tsps baking powder-pinch of black pepper-flour, all it takes-bake about 1 hour or more-350 degrees-grease pan-long glass pan

Sausage Pie a` la Caruso

2 # sausage lightly browned & drained-12 oz mozzarella-
3 hard boiled eggs (chopped fine)-2 # ricotta-4 eggs beaten-
½ cup grated cheese
Makes 2- 9" pies-350 degrees for 1 hour

**Her note...2 sticks pepperoni may be substituted for
sausage...well this one made me laugh when I compared it
to Mary Carboni's...lightly browned and drained compared
to fried...but the cheese and eggs are not light in either
recipe**

**I guess this is a filling for whatever crust you wanted to
use**

Quick Pumpkin Bread

makes 1 loaf

1 pkg (16 oz) pound cake mix-2 eggs-⅓ c milk-½ tsp nutmeg-
½ tsp cinnamon-1 cup Comstock Pumpkin Pie Filling
In large mixer bowl, combine all ingredients -blend well. Pour
into greased 9" x 5" loaf pan. Bake 1hr 15 min or until bread
springs back when lightly touched. Cool 20 min.-turn out
onto cooling rack

no temperature is noted

Corn Muffins (magazine)

¾ c softened butter
3 large eggs
2 cups milk
½ tsp salt **(omit if butter is salted)**
1 can (8 ¾ oz) whole kernel corn drained

¾ c sugar
1⅔ c flour
·4 tsp b. powder
1⅔ c corn meal

425 degree oven-2 min. or until toothpick comes out clean-
Beat sugar with butter-Beat until lite & fluffy-Beat in eggs, one at a time-beating well after each addition-Combine dry ingredients in bowl-With mixer at low speed add dry ingredients to butter mixture-alternately with milk. Begin & end with dry ingredients-Fold in corn-Bake-Cool in pan on racks 10 min., Cool completely on racks.

Spinach Turnovers (Aunt Angie's)

Pastry: 9½ c sifted flour, 2¾ c Spry, 1½ tsp salt, 2 tsps baking powder, water (about 2¼)
Bake 375 degrees for 20-30 minutes; egg wash of egg yolk & white after 10 minutes in oven
For 1 # of spinach I used 3 big Tbsps Crisco melted, 2 pinches of salt, 1 clove garlic minced, 1 to 1½ c of raisins, paprika to fill ½ of the above pastry
In the margin near Spry the note "need more than ¾ too dry"...maybe she means a little more Spry than the ¾...a little different than Carm Bono's

DRINKS, SNACKS and RELISHES

Josie and baby Julia 1926 on the backporch at 216 Fourth Ave

Grape Wine (Julia's)

2 Large cans frozen grape juice
6 Cans of water
4 Cups of sugar
½ teaspoon yeast
1 10 cent balloon

Using a small funnel, pour sugar into a glass gallon jar. Then drop in the yeast. Then pour the grape juice and water (do not need to be mixed together first). Just pour in one and then the other. Now put a very strong balloon over the top of the jug and be sure the balloon is pulled down good. Then tie a string around the top of the jug to hold the balloon on. The balloon will fill from the working of the yeast.
When the balloon has filled out and then gone down, the wine is ready to drink. This takes anywhere from 2 to 4 weeks. After it is done, put a lid on the jug and keep it on tight, the longer the wine sits the better it is. Don't shake to mix, it will work itself.

P.S. you can substitute frozen apple juice for variety

Whiskey Sour Punch

1 small orange- 3 6 oz cans frozen lemonade concentrate (thawed)-3 cups orange juice-1 fifth rye, bourbon or scotch (chilled)
1 32 oz bottle club soda-chilled
2 trays ice cubes
About 25 minutes before serving-Prepare garnish
Thinly slice orange-discard ends-With small sharp knife-flute edges of slices-set aside
In punch bowl-combine undiluted lemonade concentrate and remaining ingredients-mix well-garnish with orange slices. Makes 16 cups or three 2½ cup servings.

Tropical Punch (very good)

1-46 oz can red Hawaiian fruit punch
1-6 oz can frozen lemonade concentrate
1- 6 oz can frozen orange juice concentrate
1 -6 oz can frozen grape juice concentrate
3½ cups chilled gingerale (1 pt. 12oz bottle)
6 cups cold water

Combine the fruit punch-lemonade-orange juice-grape concentrate and water. Pour over ice in large punch bowl (use an ice ring with orange slices and fresh mint leaves frozen in it, if desired). Resting bottle on rim of punch bowl-carefully pour in gingerale (makes 30 to 35 servings)

My large punch bowl holds 10 qts. Double above recipe and add ½ qt gingerale…enuf for 1 punch bowl) Lucy has this bowl.

Lemonade

Grandma Sgroi's and Mommy's

Juice and pulp of 4 freshly squeezed lemons-2 qts water- 1 generous cup extra fine sugar-refrigerate-serve ice cold-stir well-pour over ice

Editor's note: take out the seeds or you'll have complaining kids…she use to tell me they were good for my digestion and to stop moaning…I remember Grandma put her lemonade in a 2 qt pink depression glass pitcher

Punch

for Teacher's Recognition Day Luncheon

10 scoops of lime sherbet-3 qts gingerale

sounds like she got this one when she worked in the cafeteria

Orchard Punch

1 qt water-⅓ cup loose tea or 15 tea bags-2 qts orange juice-1 qt grapefruit juice-1 qt light corn syrup-1 bottle (⁴/₅ qt) champagne (chilled)
Bring water to a rolling boil in a saucepan. Remove from heat and immediately add tea. Brew uncovered four minutes. Strain. Stir in orange juice and grapefruit juice and corn syrup. When ready to serve pour into punch bowl and add a block of ice. Stir to chill. Pour in champagne-Garnish with orange slices. Yield-circa 56- ½ cup servings

Holiday Punch

2 cups bottled apple juice-1 cup fresh frozen lemon juice-1 cinnamon stick-1 cup fresh frozen orange juice-1 cup frozen canned pineapple juice-10 whole cloves-2 cups chilled white wine-2 cups chilled sparkling water.
Mix apple juice-orange, lemon & pineapple juice together. Add cinnamon sticks and cloves. Bring mixture to a boil and cook gently, stirring occasionally for 15 min
Strain-chill until very cold. Fill cube trays half full of water-place a red or green cherry in each. Freeze until almost firm. Just before serving add chilled wine. Pour into punch bowl-add sparkling water. Add ice cubes or plain block of ice if you prefer. Serve very cold-makes 16 4 oz servings.

Café Au Lait Mix

1 6 oz jar cremora-1¼ c packed brown sugar-¼ cup instant coffee crystals-dash salt
Combine ingredients and store in air-tight container. Makes 2 cups. For 1 serving-Stir ¼ cup mix & ⅔ cup boiling water in cup. Add a cinnamon stick-stir.

Whiskey

2 cups water-1½ cup sugar-melt sugar in heavy iron skillet until golden brown-add hot water. Let cool-add 2 cups alcohol. After water is added to burnt sugar-boil until sugar is dissolved. Makes 1 qt.

Liqueurs

1½ cups sugar-6 cups water-bring to boiling point and let cool.
Add 2 cups of alcohol and 2 bottles of flavored extract. Makes 2 qts

Season's Greeting Punch

1 c sugar-2 cups Realemon juice-1 46 oz can red fruit flavored punch-chilled, 1 28 oz bottle gingerale or club soda- chilled. Maraschino cherries and orange slices (optional).
In qt measure or medium bowl-stir sugar into Realemon until dissolved. Place ice cubes I large punch bowl. Pour in Realemon & sugar mixture and red punch. Slowly add gingerale. Stir. If desired garnish with cherries & orange slices. Makes about 3 qts-or 22½ cup servings.

Orange Jupiter Mix

1¾ cups non–fat dry milk-½ c sugar-1 9 oz jar orange flavored breakfast drink powder-2 tsps vanilla
Stir together dry ingredients-Blend in vanilla-Store in air tight container. Makes about 4 cups mix
For 1 serving: Place ⅓ c orange mix-½ c cold water and 2 ice cubes in a blender-cover-blend 30 to 45 seconds or until mixture is smooth. Garnish with orange slices if desired.
For 3 servings: Place 1 cup mix-1½ c cold water in blender. Cover-blend until smooth. Add 5 or 6 ice cubes-1 cube at a time-blend until chopped after each addition.

She notes: This mix makes a drink reminiscent of an orange juice stand shake.

Orange Shake

1 c o. juice-⅓ c powdered milk (dry) 1 to 2 Tbsps sugar-½ tsp vanilla-½ c ice cubes
Place all ingredients in blender. Cover-blend until ice is crushed.

Hot Cocoa Mix

2 c Cremora-1½ c sugar-¾ c unsweetened cocoa-½ c non fat dry milk-¼ tsp salt
In large container-combine ingredients-Mix well-Store in air-tight container.
To serve-spoon 2 to 3 heaping tsps of into a mug. Add 1 c boiling water-stir.

Mocha Coca Mix-Add ¼ c instant coffee to mix.

Gift idea-Place in decorated air-tight jar.

Sangria

1 lime	3 bananas sliced
1 orange	1 bottle dry red wine (a fifth)
¼ c brandy	1 7 oz bottle carbonated water
2 Tbsps sugar	

Fruit slices and peels for garnish

Squeeze lime and orange. Pour juice into pitcher one half full of ice. Pour in brandy & sugar. Drop in banana slices-press lightly against side of pitcher with a wooden spoon. Pour wine, then soda into the pitcher. Stir-Pour into glasses garnished with fruit slices. 12-18 servings

Sangria Roja (makes 36 servings)

1 gal Burgandy wine-2 large seedless oranges (sliced)-2 lemons sliced-2 limes (sliced)-4 Tbsps sugar-ice cubes

Fill 3 (2 qt size) pitchers ⅓ full of ice cubes. Place and equal amount of fruit slices in each pitcher. Sprinkle with an equal amount of sugar. Fill pitchers about ¾ full of wine. With a wooden spoon pound fruit slices so that juices are blended thoroughly with wine & sugar. Keep refrigerated until serving time. Just before serving, press fruit slices again-add a few more ice cubes and stir before serving.

Strawberry Daiquiri

2 cups strawberries-½ c lite rum-3 Tbsps sugar-1 Tbsp lime juice-1 c crushed ice
Place berries-rum-sugar & lime juice in blender container. Cover & process on high until pureed. Add ice. Cover & blend until smooth. Serve immediately **(2 cups)**

Lipton Onion Soup Butter

Thoroughly blend 1 envelope Lipton Onion Soup Mix with 1 container (8 oz) whipped butter or soft margarine. Makes 1¼ cups. Store covered in refrigerator.

Onion buttered bread-spread between slices of French or It. Bread-wrap in foil-heat 15-20 min.

Onion buttered baked potatoes–Top a split hot baked potato with 1 to 2 Tbsps onion butter

Onion buttered corn on the cob-Spread onion butter on hot ears of corn. Butter uncooked corn and wrap in foil. Roast on outdoor grill or in 400 degree oven-30 min.

Onion buttered Minute Steaks or hamburgers- Cook minute steaks or hamburgers in hot onion butter

Onion buttered vegetables-add 2 Tbsps onion butter to a cooked and drained package (10 oz) frozen vegetables.

Onion buttered noodles-Toss ½ # cooked & drained noodles with ¼ cup onion butter

Hot Dips (Vicki)

Baked Artichoke Hearts

1 can Progresso artichoke hearts (drain)
use greased baking dish

chop hearts-add 1 cup mayonnaise-¾ cup grated cheese-stir-
Bake at 400 degrees, 10-15 min until bubbly
Serve with fancy crackers

Hot Clam Dip

2 cans minced or chopped clams with juice
½ stick melted oleo
2 cups grated mozzarella
¾ tsp garlic salt
1 tsp Oregano
1 cup bread crumbs
Mix everything but oleo in baking dish. Then melt oleo and pour over top. Bake at 350 degrees-15 min.
Serve hot with fancy crackers

Garlic Rolls (knots)

1 # regular bread dough-Let rise 2 hours. Cut off little pcs. And roll like a cigar. Tie in a knot. Put on ungreased cookie sheet. Bake at 400 degrees- 10-15 min until brown. In a bowl put ⅓ c oil-garlic salt & oregano and grated cheese-stir in baked knots hot from the oven. Add more cheese if desired.

Spinach Balls

1 pkg frozen chopped spinach-thawed & drained
6 Tbsps melted butter
3 eggs well beaten
clove garlic minced
½ tsp
dried thyme leaves
1 med. Onion finely chopped
⅓ cup grated Parmesan
1½ cups Pepperidge Farm herb stuffing
In medium bowl combine all ingredients. If mixture is too soft-add more stuffing. Form into balls about 1½ " in diameter. Place on greased cookie sheet-Bake at 350 degrees for 10 minutes (20 min) or until tan.
Serve hot-(makes about 24)

Sauerkraut Salad

Wash and drain 1 No. 2 ½ can sauerkraut. Mix with 1 cup diced celery-1 large onion chopped-1 cup diced green pepper or 1 cup grated carrots for color.

Mix together-1¼ cup sugar-½ c vinegar and ½ c salad oil and pour over the vegetables.

Souse (Pickled Pork)

4 pork hocks-1 Tbsp salt-1 rounded tsp pickling spice-1 c vinegar-½ tsp sugar
Cover hocks with cold water. Bring to a boil & simmer until tender. Remove bones from hocks & place in ceramic or glass container. Reduce stock to 2 cups. Add spices & vinegar- Boil 1 to 2 minutes. Strain. Refrigerate until jellied.

This all but gags me. My father cut up stew beef or fresh roasted pork and mix with onions, salt, vinegar and a dash of salt and sugar for sandwiches. I never remember eating this Souse stuff.

Refrigerator Summer Squash & Zucchini Pickles

3 yellow squash (1 #). 3 med zucchini (1 #). 1 lemon thinly sliced and cut in half. 1 red pepper (8 oz) sliced-½ c onion sliced. 2 tsp salt- 2 tsp celery seed-¾ c sugar-½ c lemon juice
Prepare day ahead-wash the squashes-Cut unpeeled squashes into thin slices about ⅛" thick. In large bowl combine squashes, lemon-pepper –onion-salt & celery seed. Toss gently to combine. Let stand 1 hr. In small bowl combine sugar & lemon juice-stirring until sugar is dissolved. Pour over vegetables and refrigerate covered 24 hours. To take to picnic-turn pickles into 2 qt glass jar with cover.

Her notes: Nice served as a relish with sliced cold meat loaf. These are uncooked refrigerator pickles

Cranberry Relish

Grind 1 cup fresh or frozen cranberries-3 med carrots sliced-½ c each of sliced celery and red maraschino cherries (about 20 cherries) and ¼ cup walnuts. Stir in 2 Tbsps sugar-Chill. Makes about 5 cups.

Marinade for Roasted Peppers

1½ c oil-¾ c white wine vinegar-1 tsp salt-1 Tbsp oregano-1 Tbsp basil (garlic)

that's it! How many pounds of peppers is not mentioned. I guess you could make and keep in refrig and use as desired.

Seasoning Salt (Newspaper)

This is funny. Newspaper's version and then she totally revises it!

Mix together 6 Tbsps salt-5 Tbsps pepper-5 Tbsps celery salt-5 Tbsps garlic salt-5 Tbsps onion salt-6 Tbsps Accent-Tbsps paprika.

She tried ¼ recipe to test then added–6 Tbsps grated Romano cheese-6 Tbsps sesame seed

Final recipe with her "check" written in the margin, noting that this was the final recipe.
1 Tbsp + ½ tsp salt-1 Tbsp pepper-1 Tbsp celery salt-1 Tbsp garlic salt-1 Tbsp + ½ tsp Accent-1 Tbsp + ½ tsp paprika-1 Tbsp + ½ tsp Romano cheese-1Tbsp+1tsp sesame seed-check
Isn't Accent an illegal drug now? I guess this is a dry rub for meat.

Italian Herb Blend

½ cup leaf oregano
½ cup basil
2 Tbsps sage

3¼ oz seasoned salt
2 Tbsps lemon pepper
2 Tbsps garlic powder

Mix-pack into glass jar- seal and store in cool dry place.

I'd rather go to Symeon's on Commercial Drive in Utica and buy his already to go!...Use as dry rub or in recipe below

Salad Dressing

2 cups veg oil
2 Tbsps Italian Herb Blend (above)
⅔ cup red wine vinegar
¼ cup grated Romano cheese
2 cloves garlic chopped
1 tsp cracked pepper
Beat with wire whisk until thick and blended-Refrigerate

1 Tbsp sugar
1 Tbsp salt

Basic Dressing

⅓ c lemon juice-⅔ c salad oil-1 Tbsp fresh chopped basil (or 1 tsp dried basil) –½ tsp salt-½ tsp sugar-¼ tsp pepper-Combine all ingredients in jar with tight fitting cover-shake vigorously. Refrigerate covered 2 hrs. Makes 1 cup

Antipasta Salad

1 jar marinated artichokes-1 c sliced pepperoni-4 slices of provolone cut in half- 1 lge tomato cut in wedges-1 small cuke peeled & sliced. Line platter with lettuce leaves-remaining ingredients placed attractively around platter-Just before serving, place marinated artichokes on platter

31

Bar BQ sauce

(may be used to baste chops, steaks chicken & kabobs)

1 envelope Onion Soup Mix-1½ c water-1 cup catsup-¼ tsp garlic powder-1 tsp Worcestershire sauce
Combine all ingredients in saucepan. Bring to a boil. Simmer 10 min. stirring frequently-makes 2 cups sauce

Aunt Angie's Bar BQ Sauce

¼ c oil-¾ c chopped onion-¾ c ketchup-¾ c water-⅓ c lemon juice-3 Tbsps sugar-3 Tbsps Worcestershire sauce-2 Tbsp Prepared Mustard-2 tsps salt-½ tsp blk pepper
Simmer 15-20 min

Pickled green Tomatoes (Rose Guarniere)

1 hand basket full of green tomatoes...now there is an exact measurement!!
1. Slice green tomatoes-salted for 3 days. (Put heavy object on top) Drain
2. Keep in white vinegar overnight and drain
3. In large pan mix in with tomatoes: 1 cup parsely-½ cup fennel seed-1 cup chopped garlic-½ cup oregano-and hot or sweet green and red peppers (1 qt chopped peppers)

Mix altogether-put in jars-fill with oil to the top & close

Revisions...but of course!!! In '73-1 good hand basket makes 12 pints
¼ cup chopped garlic instead of full cup
'79 –I used ¼ c oregano
¼ c chopped garlic

Green Tomato Pickles (Sammy T-Baker employee)

Green tomatoes-fennel seed-hot peppers-pure salt-1 clean crock(sterilized)

Wash tomatoes in cold water. Remove brown spots & slice thin-Arrange 2 inch layer in crock. Sprinkle fennel seed-3 slices of hot pepper-3 garlic cloves. Apply salt generously. Repeat until crock is full.
Cover with china dish (glass pie plate) & something heavy to hold it down. Skim off every week. Ready in 4-8 weeks. Never add water at any time.
Follow up recipe
Wash tomatoes and drain. To every quart of tomatoes add ⅓ cup oil and season with crushed pepper & oregano. Place in jars-seal and keep in cool place.

Revision in 1973 "check" read below

Green tomatoes (salted). Slice green tomatoes and salt-in crock-When almost full-place glass pie dish with a weight on it to keep tomato slices under liquid. 3 days later drain-pack in jars-pour hot water to fill jars. Process about (20-30 min) in boiling water. Remove from canner lower wire. Cool & store.

She lost me on this revision...fried green tomatoes are much easier!...my father worked for Baker's Greenhouse...sounds like she got it from someone who worked there

Wine Jelly

1 c Burgundy wine-1½ c sugar-stir until sugar melts and comes to a rolling boil. Remove from heat and add 1 bottle of Certo-Pour into glasses-Seal-May be doubled

Strawberry Pineapple Jam

4 c prepared fruit-7 cups sugar-½ bottle Certo-Use one No. 2 can crushed pineapple. Mix with 1 qt crushed fully ripe strawberries (should measure 4 cups). Place in large saucepan (stainless or enamel) Add sugar to fruit. Mix well. Place over very high heat-<u>bring to a full rolling boil </u>and<u> boil hard one minute</u> stirring constantly. Remove from heat and at once- stir in Certo. Stir & skim for 5 minutes. Ladle quickly into glasses. Parraffin at once (about 10-6 oz glasses)

prepared fruit ...what does that mean ...cut fresh fruit?... I'm not a canner

Hot Artichoke Dip

1 can artichoke hearts-3 pkgs frozen drained spinach-Chop artichoke hearts and mix with spinach-place in greased (olive oil) 8 x 10" pan-Then spread the following mixture over the spinach and artichokes
Beat 8 oz cream cheese-2 Tbsps mayonaisse-6 Tbsps of milk and a dash of pepper-Sprinkle with Italian cheese-Bake at 375 degrees for 40 min

Refrigerator Style Dill Pickles (Antoinette)

Use gallon jar-Put dill on bottom-Slice cucumbers thin-do not peel-put garlic here and there
Make solution as follows: 1 qt. White vinegar-2 cups sugar-½ cup salt-2 scant Tbsps blk pepper-8 cloves garlic-about 3, 4 or 5 sprigs of dill-Stir all ingredients until dissolved-Cover tightly-Keep in refrigerator-do not heat anything-Takes about 1 week or more.

Chili Sauce (Mrs. Harvey's) next door neighbor

18 ripe tomatoes
3 sweet green peppers
1 good sized onion
1 tsp cinnamon
(tied in a bag)

1 cup sugar
2 tsps salt
1 cup vinegar
1 tsp allspice

Combine the vegetables, salt and sugar-Cook until mixture begins to thicken-then add vinegar and whole spices and cook until mixture becomes a thick sauce. Pour into hot jars & seal immediately.

Note: drain juice from vegetables before adding vinegar-shortens cooking period... Mrs. Harvey was Grandma Sgroi's nextdoor neighbor in the 1930's

Golden Glow Pickles

12 large cucumbers-2 tsps celery seed-6 large onions sliced-2 tsps tumeric-3 cups vinegar-2 Tbsps white mustard seed-1 cup water-2 cups sugar

Pare cucumbers and quarter-cut off seeds-Soak cucumbers and onions overnight in brine-Drain-Combine remaining ingredients-Cook 5 minutes-Add cucumbers and onions-Heat to boiling point-Seal in hot sterilized jars (6 pts)

Brine: 1 cup salt to 4 quarts of water

Notes: In 1973 I used this recipe but I used green cucumbers (did not peel them) and 1 bunch of celery cut up (I used brown sugar)-made 1½ times the recipe

I had to triple vinegar to cover pickles while bringing to a boil-makes 14 pints

Sweet Cucumber Pickles (Mrs. Harvey's)

1 qt sliced cucumbers}
1 handful small onions} Sprinkle with salt-let stand 3 hours

Drain and add 1 cup brown sugar-20 cloves-1 tsp tumeric-
1 Tbsps whole mustard seed-1 Tbsps chopped horse radish-
enough vinegar to cover-Heat do not boil

Chunk Pickles

1 qt small onions	1 head cauliflower
1 qt green tomatoes	2 red peppers
1 qt cucumbers	1 cup salt

Let stand in brine over night-2 qts vinegar-2 cups sugar-
2 Tbsps mixed spices-Heat together-can hot

I guess you have to know how to can to use this recipe

English Pickled eggs

12 hard cooked eggs-cider vinegar-1 tsp mixed picking spices-
beet juice (optional) may be added to give them a pink color-
Leave in jars one month or more
Serve as an appetizer or with cold meats

Mixed Pickles

2 qts small cucumbers-3 red peppers-3 green peppers-2 qts
small pickling onions-1 bunch celery-2 cups brown sugar-
3 qts vinegar-1 pkg pickling spices
Wash and dry cucumbers-Cut peppers in strips-peel onions-
cut celery-Soak vegetables in 1 cup salt and 4 qts water
overnite-Drain thoroughly. Mix.

Zucchini Pickles

5 # zucchini sliced thin
3 red onions
½ cup salt
3 trays of ice cubes
3 cups white vinegar
3 cups white sugar
2 tsps celery seed
2 tsps mustard
1½ tsps turmeric
1½ tsps ginger
1½ tsps black pepper

Combine zucchini-onions & salt in a bowl-Top with layer of ice cubes-Let stand 3 hours-Drain-Rinse zucchini & onions in cold water-Combine with vinegar & sugar & spices & heat to boiling-Reduce heat-Simmer 2 min-Pack while hot in hot sterilized jars. Makes 5 pints

Note: when topping zucchini with ice-"work in ice cubes."... a little more of a hint on how to pickle...maybe pick yourself up a book on pickling ...I'm a Vlasic girl myself.

Pickled Peppers (½bushel of peppers)

1 gal vinegar}
2 qts water}
½ cup salt}   let these come to a boil

Fill jars with peppers & cloves of garlic. Add 1 tsp oregano and a scant ½ tsp alum (for crisper peppers)

Pickled Pepper Salad

Combine 2 Tbsps oil-2 Tbsps vinegar-¼ tsp pepper-⅛ tsp salt-¼ tsp oregano-Toss with 2 cups sliced pickled peppers-¾ c chopped celery-½ c ripe olives, sliced-8 anchovy fillets chopped. Serve cold

This recipe assumes that the peppers you pickled actually became pickled peppers

Finger Salad with Dunking Sauce

Use cold crisp vegetables-red & white radishes-small green onions-Romaine-cucumber sticks-peeled & halved small carrots-sprigs of watercress-thinly sliced turnips-use the following sauce

Remoulade

1 c sour cream-1 c mayonaisse-¼ c chopped capers-1 minced garlic clove-3 Tbsps chopped chives-1½ tsps paprika-1 Tbsp chopped fresh dill or 2 Tbsps chopped dill pickles-1 Tbsp lemon juice-2 Tbsp chopped parsley. Blend all ingredients-let mellow for 1 or 2 hrs. Makes about 2½ cups of sauce.

Caponata (Aunt Angie's)
Eggplant appetizer

2 large eggplants peeled & diced-2 cups celery diced-2 large onions minced-1-5 oz bottle pimento stuffed olives-about 6-8 cups of peppers (cut up)-1 Tbsp capers (optional)-1 Tbsp fresh parsley chopped- about 1 cup tomato puree or sauce-oil for frying

Sauté celery until soft (about 7 minutes)-remove from pan and drain-sauté onions until soft-remove from pan and drain-do the same with peppers-sauté eggplant until soft (about 10 minutes) and drain well, (eggplant soaks up a lot of oil). In a stainless steel pan add ⅓ cup red wine vinegar-1 Tbsp sugar-tomato puree, cover and simmer about 15 minutes-add eggplant-celery-peppers-parsley-olives-capers and simmer 10 more minutes-will keep 1 week or 10 days in refrigerator in a covered container-or may be frozen

****

COOKIES

Josephine in 1930 high school graduation photo

Frances Izzo's Italian Cookies ($1.50)

5 # flour-1 doz eggs (room temp) 8 Tbsps b. powder- 2 # sugar-1 # Spry (room temp) as much milk (about 1 cup) as it takes (lukewarm) vanilla (about 4 Tbsps)

Make a well with dry ingredients-add remaining ingredients and mix thoroughly-make into rolls-then brush with beaten egg-bake-then slice diagonally-may top with sesame seeds-For anise cookies add anise seed-Bake in 375 degree 4 minutes on bottom shelf-5 minutes on top shelf

She has this note: this may be used for cuchidata (recipe for cuchidata found later in this section)
¼ of recipe
5 c flour-3 eggs-2 Tbsps b. powder-½ c shortening-about ¼ cup milk-1 Tbsp vanilla-1½ c sugar
 she tried 1¼ cup but decided on recheck that 1½ cups was needed; also in 1988 she made half lemon and half vanilla... and made 72 cookies...did this recipe cost $1.50 in 1988... this must be a 1950's cost
Frances lived across the street from us when we lived on Palmer and 4th in the early 1950's

Cherry Chip Cookies

very good makes 25 cookies
½ cup shortening (part butter)-½ cup sugar-1 egg-1 tsp vanilla- 1½ cups flour-¼ tsp soda-½ tsp soda-½ tsp salt-⅓ cup walnuts-⅓ cup cherry chips
Mix together shortening-sugar-egg & vanilla. Add sifted flour-soda and salt. Add nuts-cherry chip. Drop rounded tsp 2" apart on lightly greased cookie sheet. Bake until delicately browned-8-10 min 375 degrees. Cookies should be still soft. Cool slightly-then remove from cookie sheet

Cherry Nut Cookies (Mary Lore's) $1.11

Beat 1 cup Spry-1¼ cups sugar-½ tsp salt until creamy-add 3 eggs-½ tsp almond flavoring-1 cup cherry juice-blend-add 5½ cups flour sifted with 3 Tbsps b. powder. Beat and add ½ cup chopped nuts and small bottle of chopped-drained maraschino cherries. 350 degrees-10 min-ungreased cookie sheets-about 90-110 cookies.

She notes: if cherry juice is lacking add enough milk to make a cup...was written to bake at 375 degrees...this was checked and changed to 350...to bake 5 min on low (2nd) notch and 5 min on hi (4th notch)...the notch is the level in her oven...second baking was for 6 min...low for 5 min... this recipe has been perfected by her. Me, I just throw them in the oven on my cooking stone and take them out when they smell done...no timer !!

Brownies a`la Aunt Julia

13x9x2 pan
1 pkg choc cake mix-¼ c water-2 eggs-¼ c shortening, oil or melted or softened butter or oleo (some kinda fat!!) ¼ c packed brown sugar or ⅓ c granulated sugar-½ c chopped nuts. Blend ½ of cake mix (**dry**)-water-egg & shortening & sugar in a bowl-Mix thoroughly. Blend in remaining cake mix-Stir in nuts, spread in pan.
Glaze: xxxx sugar-choc syrup-little water or milk. Bake 350 for 25 min.
greased pan

Almond Paste Cookies

(Mary Dip-Mary Sylvester) $1.28
3 egg whites beaten-1 lb kernel paste-1¾ c verifine sugar-Grate the paste-add sugar–mix thoroughly-Beat egg whites until foamy. Mix thoroughly-Place on greased pans bake at 350 degrees-15 to 20 min. Bake one pan at a time-have a rack in middle of oven. Let cookies rest about 5 min. before removing from pan

Almond Paste Cookies (Angie Sassone) $3.15

2½ lb kernel paste (grated) 1¼ cups xxxx sugar-1¼ cups sugar-10 Tbsps flour-10 egg whites beaten.
Mix but do not over beat-add coloring-cut brown paper size of pan-grease pan & paper-Bake 10 to 15 min-350 degrees
This note: (Put thru cookie press-Remove from paper immediately)...is this after they are baked before while or during...do they sabotage these recipes so no one can bake them. Angie Sassone is Aunt Angie.

Almond Paste Cookies (Mary Lore) $1.30

1 lb kernel paste (grated) 1 lb sugar-14 rounded Tbsps bread crumbs **(I tripled recipe and used 2 cups bread crumbs)** 3 egg whites beaten but not too stiff-1 drop of food coloring-Make them round-dip in sugar and place on greased, floured pan about 12 min in 350 degree oven-watch carefully-do not let brown-remove when cool (70 cookies)

In the margin she has 1 # paste and ⅔ c bread crumbs

Almond Cookies (Mary Valente) $1.04

1 # shelled almonds (ground)-1 lb sugar-3 eggs-½ tsp cloves-½ tsp cinnamon-juice of ½ lemon-lemon rind (1 lemon)-tangerine rind (½). Mix almonds and sugar-Make a well-Add eggs & remaining ingredients. Bake in 350 degrees. Line pan with brown paper. Let cool awhile before removing from pan (or bottom will leave on paper)

well there you have it-4 great female baking talents from Frankfort, New York making almond cookies...I'm lost on the brown paper thing I've never baked with brown paper... I have learned these cookies should cool before removing them...what is up with this cost analysis

Chinese Chews (Mary Jane Kinney)

2 eggs well beaten-1 cup sugar-¼ tsp salt-1 cup finely chopped dates-1 cup finely chopped nuts-¾ c cake flour-1 tsp b. powder
Beat eggs-add sugar-beat well. Sift dry ingredients-add dates & nuts-add flour mixture. Line pan with wax paper.
350 degrees-bout 40 min. Sprinkle with xxxx sugar
cut while warm
this note in margin...pan size?...Mary Jane Kinney was our neighbor when I was in high school.

Easter or Christmas Rolls (Aunt Angie's)

12 eggs-12 tsps b. powder-2 cups sugar-3 tsps vanilla-1 cup oil-8 cups flour (more if needed) 1 cup orange juice
Mix oil and sugar-add eggs-mix-add flour & dry ingredients. Mix thoroughly-Roll to ¼ " and fill or make cookies or Easter bread*
Filling for above: chop 1 pkg dates-1 # walnuts-Soak 1 pkg figs until soft for 10 min. Cool-spread on rolled dough-fold over filling-(1 long roll). Bake-when cool cut(slice) as needed

My comment: I guess the figs are soaked in very warm water, are probably chopped as well when cooled...and the dates, walnuts and figs are mixed well before being spread on the rolled dough. *Also you can make the filled cookies or just use the pastry for an Easter bread...not very clear

Cookies for Vicki's shower

found this entry in her cook book
Mrs. Longo's soft cookies sesame seed
2 batches my recipe Fig nut pinwheels
Almond paste-3 batches
Choc spice-1 batch-Betty Crocker's
Cherry winks-2 batches
Eggy-1 batch-Mary's recipe
Mrs. Barretta's cookies-1 batch
Satin glazed date drops-4 batches
Butter horns-1 batch
Thumbprint-1 batch
Golden nugget-2 batches-Cookie Cookbook

Betty Crocker's Easy Sugar Cookies

1 c sugar-1 c oleo or butter softened-1 egg-2 tsps vanilla-2 c flour-½ tsp b. soda-½ tsp cream of tarter

Mix first 4 ingredients-then stir in remaining ingredients. Cover & refrigerate 1 hr or longer. Shape into 1" balls. Dip cookie stamps or bottom of a glass into sugar and flatten rolls on ungreased cookie sheet. Bake 8 min at 330 degrees-4 min bottom shelf-4 minutes on top rack. About 50 cookies.

Italian Chocolate Filled Cookies

4 cups unsifted flour-3 eggs beaten-½ cup sugar-4 tsp b. powder-¾ c oil-½ c milk-2 tsp vanilla-Mix the above together

Filling 1 can condensed milk-8oz chopped walnuts-12 oz pkg choc chips-1 tsp vanilla. Melt choc chips in milk-add vanilla & nuts-Pat ½ of the dough in pan. Spread filling over pastry-then roll other ½ dough and put on top of filling-350 degrees 25 min in a 9x13" pan-In a 10x13" pan-350 degrees 20-25 min **Following note: need at least ¼ to ½ more of flour...does she mean cup...I would guess ⅔ of recipe**

3 c flour-2 eggs-⅔ c sugar-½ c oil-2⅔ tsp b. powder-⅓ c milk-1⅓ tsp vanilla

In the margin: in 1995 I omitted the water and used a 13x9" pan... no water in the above recipe so this must be the revised recipe

Pizza Cuisi

8 cups flour-4 lge eggs-2 tsp vanilla-3 or 4 tsps b.powder-2 # lard **(good Italian measure)**-1 cup water (plus)
Roll dough-put oil on crust-rub all over-add a little honey. Sprinkle with sugar & cinnamon-Cut in strips (about 2½ " wide) Sprinkle with nuts & raisin filling on half of the strip. Fold over other half-roll into a rosette. **Instead of lining pan with dough-I lined it with greased aluminum foil**
Filling: 2 # chopped walnuts-1 tangerine peel-2 boxes raisins-honey. Bake 350 degrees about 1 hr (check before)-Pour honey over the pizza cuisi before baking. When it starts to brown pour more honey over it
In 1989 I used 1 box raisins & 1 lb chopped nuts-tangerine peel-I made 4 pizzas
1 8" pie pan-1 ring-1 9" pie pan-1 9" round pan

How about that a recipe that calls for 2 # of lard in the recipe and still needs to be rubbed with oil before placing filling on it!

Light Brownies (good for Christmas)

2¼ c flour-1¼ tsp salt-1 c butter or oleo softened-1¼ c sugar-1 egg-1 tsp vanilla-
12 oz choc chips (2 cups) 1 c chopped nuts-maraschino cherries, drained and pat dry
Combine flour-b.powder & salt
In bowl combine butter & sugar-beat until creamy-Add egg-vanilla-mix well-gradually blend in flour mix-Stir in chips & nuts. Spread in greased 13x9" glass baking dish-Press 30 cherries into dough-spacing them to form 6 rows, 5 per row. Place 2 quartered spearmint leaves at base of each cherry. Press into dough-Bake at 350 degrees 25-30 min. Cool-cut into 2" squares-30 squares

Josie's Recipe Collection:

Kleiner's (Ma S.)

Beat 6 egg yolks and 2 whole eggs with ¼ lb of sugar-2 Tbsps cream-3 Tbsps melted butter-mix with as much as a pound of flour-as much that can be stirred into it-Knead the mixture with the remaining flour until the dough no longer sticks to hands or the board. Roll out onto floured board until it is thin. Cut lengthwise-slit in the middle and pull one end through the slit- so the cookies become twisted in the middle. Fry in deep hot fat until brown. Makes about 100 small kleiners.
Velbe komme...Grandma Sgroi's recipe...don't believe these ever made an impression on me

Rosettes (Aunt Mary's)

5 or 6 eggs-½ cup melted lard-½ cup water-as much flour as it will take up (about 6 cups sifted flour) Roll thin-cut in strips and pinch together and roll to make rosette-Serve with powdered sugar or honey (add 1 tsp baking powder-makes them less crisp)
For pingiolotti-boil honey about 10 min.

Rosettes (Nana's)

7 eggs-1 heaping tsp b. powder-3 good cups of flour
**well, velbe komme to you!...how do we cook these babies...
I believe rosettes are deep fried...place on paper toweling...
honey and/or powdered sugar when cool**

Dessert Rosettes

2 eggs slightly beaten   1 cup milk
2 tsps sugar   1 cup flour
¼ tsp salt   1 tbsp lemon extract

Add sugar to slightly beaten eggs-then add milk. Sift flour before measuring-then sift together with salt. Stir to first mixture and beat until smooth (about the consistency of heavy cream)-Add flavoring

Dip iron into hot fat in a deep kettle, to heat it-then drain excess fat on brown paper. Fat should be hot enough to brown a piece of bread while counting to sixty. Dip heated iron in batter-not to more than ¾ its height. If only a thin batter adheres to the iron-dip it again until a smooth layer forms. It will be partly cooked from the heat of the iron. Plunge batter coated iron quickly into hot fat-cook 2-3 min (until active bubbling ceases) Remove from iron and drain on brown paper. If your rosettes are not crisp- the batter is to thick and should be diluted with milk while still warm. Dip in xxxx sugar

I think Lucy sold these irons at the yard sale...we looked at them while cleaning the kitchen and barely knew what they were...and threw them in the sale box...I wonder if anybody bought them

Cannoli a la Palermitani (Mary Cross)

2 cups flour-4 Tbsps butter (⅛ #)-2 tsps sugar-4 Tbsps milk (¼ cup)-1½ Tbsp lemon juice-grated rind of ½ lemon

Melt butter-sift flour-add sugar-lemon juice and butter. Add milk slowly. Let rest awhile-Roll thin-roll on pins and fry in deep fat (about 20 min)-Put a little egg yolk on points to hold together while frying

She notes: 35 cannoli when I roll them out one by one...
**detailed cannoli recipe next page

Molasses Cookies (Alta's)

1 c br. sugar   1 cup molasses
1 c shortening   ½ tsp salt
*3 tsps (heaping) b. soda }   1 tsp ginger
*1 tsp powdered alum}
*place b. soda and alum in ⅔ c boiling water and enough flour
to make dough-let stand overnight

**she notes: about 4 cups of flour...that's it...end of recipe...
make it happen yourself**

Alta's Potato Fudge Bars

1 c sugar-3 Tbsps cocoa-½ c shortening or oil-2 eggs-1 tsp
vanilla-½ c sifted flour-1 tsp b. soda-2 Tbsps milk-¼ tsp
vinegar-1 c grated raw potato (pat dry) 1 c nuts
8x8" pan 350 degrees

Cannoli (Mc Calls Magazine)

Shells:

3 c sifted flour-1 Tbsp sugar-¼ tsp cinnamon-¾ c white wine or port-1 egg yolk slightly beaten-salad oil or shortening for frying

Sift flour with sugar & cinnamon onto a board. Make a well in center & fill with wine. With a fork gradually blend flour into the liquid. When dough is firm enuf to handle-knead about 10 min or until dough is smooth & stiff (if moist & sticky knead in a little more flour)

Refrigerate dough, covered, 2 hrs. For regular sized cannoli-divide the dough into thirds. On a lightly floured surface with a stockinette covered rolling pin, roll one part of the dough to paper thinness making a rectangle slightly larger than 16x18". Trim to these dimensions. Cut into 8- 4" squares

Place a cannoli tube diagonally on a square. Wrap pastry around tubes, one corner over the other. Seal with some of the egg yolk. Repeat with remaining cannoli tubes

(keep the unused dough covered with wax paper or a damp towel so it doesn't dry out)

Meanwhile in a deep fat fryer, electric skillet or heavy saucepan, heat oil (3 or 4 inches deep) to 375 degrees. Gently drop dough covered tubes, no more than a few at a time, into hot oil & fry about 1 minute or until lightly browned on all sides (turn forms so they brown evenly). The cannoli shells should be blistered in appearance. With tongs or slotted utensil, lift the tubes out of the oil, and immediately slide off the pastry shell, the tubes will be hot-we used a pair of pointed pliers to grasp the edge so the shell could be gently pushed off with a fork. Drain shells on paper towels. Allow the tubes to cool and wipe off any oil before using again. Makes 24 cannoli shells. May be made a day or 2 ahead and stored covered at room temp-fill about 1 hour before serving.

Josie's Recipe Collection:

Filling:

3 # ricotta-2½ c xxxx sugar-4 Tbsps chopped citron-½ tsp cinnamon

for chocolate filling-2 squares melted semi sweet chocolate

Garnish-chopped citron-grated sweet choc-chopped pistachio nuts-xxxx sugar **(optional)**

Beat ricotta cheese 1 min-add 2½ cups xxxx sugar and beat until light & creamy-about 1 min.-add chopped citron & cinnamon & beat at low speed until blended. Refrigerate covered until chilled (at least 2 hrs)

Makes 5 ½ c filling

To make choc filling, evenly divide the ricotta & sugar mixture-set ½ aside-beat the melted choc into the other half

Fill shells with small spatula from one end & then the other, press filling in gently

Garnish with grated choc, pistachio nuts or citron

Can fill half of shell with choc and half with vanilla

My kids just like the vanilla filling with choc chips mixed in...serve with whipped cream and choc drizzle or shavings...just like Little Italy...right Kimmy Ann

**Another recipe for cannoli filling toward the end of this section...I stumbled across it long after this page was typed

Shoe Taps (Rose B.)

Bake 350 degrees-8-10 min-3 c flour-1 c shortening-1½ tsps
b. powder-1 c sugar-1 tsp salt-2 eggs-½ c molasses-add raisins-
nuts or coconut-roll long like meatball croquette
**Another one of those simplistic recipes for an A student in
Cuisine**

Sfeenja (Mary Cross)

2 cups flour-2 beaten eggs-1 rounded Tbsp sugar-¼ tsp baking
powder-1 tsp of yeast-milk, enough to make soft batter-Beat
well after all ingredients are together-Let stand in warm place
until double in bulk-Fry in deep hot fat-dropping from a
teaspoon

**To triple recipe use 1 pkg of yeast dissolved in ¼ cup warm
water**

Chocolate Covered Peanut Butter Balls

1 stick margarine
1 box powdered sugar
1 18 oz jar peanut butter
blend these 3 together

Add 3 cups Rice Krispies crushed-shape into balls-melt
together in double boiler-2 large (8 oz) Hershey bars-⅓ chunk
paraffin wax-dip balls in chocolate-place on waxed paper
**I'm not sure about the paraffin thing...I think I would just
use chocolate**

Chocolate Cherry Bars

Base
1 pkg choc cake mix
21 oz can cherry pie filling
1 tsp almond extract
2 eggs beaten
Frosting
1 cup sugar
5 Tbsps oleo or butter
⅓ cup milk
1 cup (6 oz) choc chips (semi sweet)
Preheat oven to 350 degrees-grease and flour a 15 x 10" jelly roll pan or a 13 x 9 x 2" pan-In a large bowl combine base ingredients-Stir by hand until well mixed-pour into pan-bake jelly roll pan 20-30 min-13 x 9 pan 25-30

Frosting-In small saucepan combine sugar-oleo and milk-Boil stirring constantly for 1 minute-Remove from heat-stir in choc chips until smooth. Pour over warm bars
Makes 36 bars

Zeppoli

4 eggs
4 Tbsps sugar
2 lb ricotta
1 tsp vanilla
mix these together
2½ cups sifted flour
4 tsps baking powder
Fry in deep oil-drop one teaspoon full of dough at a time
Not sure about the flour...there was a hole in the paper...I wish you could see this recipe...just a scrap piece of paper that is yellowed and brittle

Egg Cookies (Abie) $1.20 plain/$1.45 frosted

12 eggs-12 cups flour-½ cup b.powder-1 cup sugar-1 cup oil-
2 tsps vanilla-all the flour it will take (10 to 11 cups)-roll out-
tie in knot-375 degree oven-bake in oven about....**that's it no
time in recipe...just blank**

**½ batch makes about 60 cookies...instead of a knot may also
just cross over...**

**these are my favorite...I bake until just a slight toast of
color...these dry fast...freeze immediately and frost when
thawed...are almost stale the next day...she doesn't say but
puts a vanilla frosting on these...butter, powdered sugar,
vanilla, enough milk to make a drizzle...leave out only what
will be consumed that day...my suggestion any way**

Italian Cookies (slices) 60 cents/with walnuts 75 cents

2 cups flour-2 tsps b. powder-½ tsp salt-1 cup sugar-3 eggs-
½ cup melted shortening-2 tsp vanilla-½ tsp anise flavoring
1 cup walnuts-Beat until shiny-Add more flour if needed-
shape into a loaf-bake 375 degrees 25 min or until lightly
browned-cool-slice

Orange Anise Cookies (Carm Bono) $1.96

3¾ c Spry-5 cups sugar-12 eggs-3 grated oranges*-18 tsp b. powder-18 cups flour-¼ tsp <u>anise oil</u>-1 tsp almond flavoring-375 to 400 degrees-5 min bottom shelf-5 min top shelf
this is a spritz cookie...use No. 1 cookie disc-No. 5 disc-thicker cookie

⅓ recipe-makes 3 # cookies
1¼ c Spry-1⅔ c sugar-4 eggs-6 tsp. b. powder-6 c flour-⅓ tsp almond flavoring-¾ tsp anise flavoring
notes in margin regarding oranges: in full recipe-1½ c orange juice + 2 to 3 Tbsps orange peel
for ⅓ recipe-½ c orange juice + 2 to 3 tsps dried orange peel...
she has dried crossed out on the full recipe...I assume she just overlooked crossing it out on the ⅓ recipe...
also note the anise oil and flavoring and the difference in amount used

Beacon Hill Cookies (Carm Trimboli)

1 cup choc chips melted-3 egg whites-½ cup sugar-pinch of salt-½ tsp vanilla-½ tsp vinegar-½ cup walnuts chopped-2 cups coconut
Beat egg whites, add sugar-beat until stiff-Add vinegar-vanilla and salt-Add cooled melted chocolate chips-walnuts & coconut. Drop with a spoon on greased cookie sheet-Bake at 375 degrees 10 to 12 min-when cool, sprinkle with xxxx sugar

My kids loved these...like chocolate candy

Anise Cookies (Mrs. Barretta-Mary Cross)

4 eggs-1 lb confectioners sugar-1 tsp anise flavoring-2 rounded tsp b. powder-1 lb flour
Mix at night lets stand a half an hour-roll them about 1" diameter-then flatten-cut at an angle about 1" long-Let stand 8 hours-Bake in 350 degree oven
Don't let them get brown

Horns (M.J. Kinney)

<u>Crust</u>-6 cups flour-1½ cups oleo-1½ c milk-1 big yeast cake
<u>Nut filling</u>-2½ c ground walnuts-1 c sugar-enough milk (⅜ cup) to make them stick

Cut shortening into flour-very fine-Heat milk to lukewarm & dissolve yeast in milk. Pour into flour mixture & mix-Roll into small meatball shape. Let rise for a couple of minutes. Roll out and fill with nut filling. Hot oven (400 degrees to 425)-watch them until they are light brown (about 10 min) Cool-Roll in xxxx sugar-Bake 5 min lower (3rd notch) and 5 min upper (5th notch)

Her note: in 1987 2½ c mixed nuts-filberts-almonds-walnuts- 1 c sugar-⅜ c milk

Brazil Nut Drops (Mother Sgroi)

½ c butter-½ c Spry-1 cup sugar-2 eggs-2¼ cups flour-¼ tsp salt-½ tsp b. soda- 2cups Brazil nut meats (cut each nut in 3 pieces) ½ tsp vanilla-½ cup moist shredded coconut
Cream sugar and shortening-blend in beaten eggs-add flour-salt & soda, sifted together-then nuts-coconut & vanilla-Drop by teaspoon on baking sheet-350 degree oven 15 min
Baking sheet-lightly greased-7 min bottom shelf 5 minutes top

Makes 45 cookies

Nut Snowballs

6 Tbsps sugar-1½ sticks oleo-2 tbsps ice water-2 tsps vanilla-2½ cups flour-1 cup pecans crushed
Cream sugar & butter-add remaining ingredients to from a stiff dough-Shape into bite sized balls-Bake at 300 degrees-20 minutes-Cool and roll in powdered sugar

Butter Coconut Tartlets

Pastry

2½ c sifted flour	1⅓ cups butter softened
½ tsp salt	2 eggs well beaten
⅔ c sugar	

Filling

2 eggs	7 oz pkg flaked coconut
1⅓ cups sugar	

Sift flour with salt and ⅔ c sugar-Cut in butter until mixture resembles coarse crumbs-Stir in beaten eggs and blend well-Knead dough slightly-Cover & refrigerate about 20 min-Preheat oven to 375 degrees-For each tartlet place 1 heaping Tbsp dough in ungreased muffin pan-Press and shape to form pastry shell-Spoon 1 Tbsp filling into each tartlet shell-Bake at 375 degrees for 22 to 24 minutes-Cool slightly, before gently removing tartlets from pans
Filling-Beat eggs well-Add sugar and coconut-Mix until thoroughly blended-Fill pastry shells as directed above
2 dozen tartlets

Raisin or Choc Chip Cookie (school recipe)

1 cup oleo-1½ cups sugar-½ cup water-3½ cups flour-1 Tbsps + b. powder-⅔ tsp salt-2 tsps vanilla-3 eggs-raisins or choc chips (6 oz)
375 degree oven-10 min-grease pan-cut as bar cookies

Soft Sugar Cookies

1 c sugar

1 c brown sugar

2 eggs

1 tsp nutmeg

2 tsps b. powder

1 tsp cream of tartar

¾ tsp salt

1 c buttermilk

½ c oleo or butter

½ c shortening

1 tsp vanilla

½ tsp lemon extract

3½ c sifted flour

¾ tsp b. soda

¾ tsp b soda

⅓ c sugar

Cream together sugar & shortening-beat in eggs-vanilla & lemon extract-Sift together dry ingredients-Add alternately with buttermilk and creamed mixture-Drop by Tbsp 2½" apart onto greased cookie sheet-425 degrees-8 min

Wine Drops (Carm Bono)

½ cup Spry-½ cup brown sugar-½ cup molasses-1 egg-½ cup milk or coffee-1 tsp b. soda-½ cup raisins-2 heaping cups of flour-variations: roll out on floured board-cut-flip into granulated sugar or xxxx sugar, add a dab of jelly on cookies flipped in xxxx sugar-or cut out and brush with egg and milk

She notes: Recipe tripled makes about 48 good sized cookies...that's all she wrote...no more...guess temp and time...and good luck!

Chocolate Filled Cookies (Mary Kinney)

<u>(Roll)</u>
(Crust $0.28)

3 cups flour-½ cup brown sugar-1 egg-½ tsp salt—⅔ cup shortening-⅓ cup milk-2½ tsps b. powder
Mix crust as you would for pie-Roll out like pie crust-spread filling-roll up like a jelly roll
Note: Divide pastry into 6 pieces-roll out each one and fill
Bake in 350 degree oven until lightly browned (about 20 Min.)-Cool and slice

The following note: (pastry needed-1 and ½ times the recipe)...haven't a clue what it means...with the amount of filling the dough recipe isn't enough?...try it out and see

Filling for above ($1.00)

2 pkgs semi sweet choc chips-**(use Nestlé's chips)**-1 can condensed milk-½ cup chopped nuts
Melt chips in double boiler-add milk and nuts-spread thin on rolled dough

These notes in the margin: Phyllis' shower-350 degrees-baked rolls 8 min bottom-8 min top-cut strips about 3"-(next time cut wider 4½"?)...I don't believe she is talking about slicing the baked rolls here...these are usually sliced about 1" after they are baked...two puzzles here...bake and solve the mystery

Drop Cookies (Mary Valent) 31 cents

⅓ cup shortening-½ cup sugar-⅓ cup milk-2 cups flour-¼ tsp salt-1 tsp b. powder-1 tsp flavoring-1 egg-½ cup nut meats cream butter, add sugar slowly-cream well-add beaten egg-add flavoring to milk-sift together dry ingredients-add alternately with milk & flavoring—add nuts-Drop by teaspoons on greased cookie sheet-Bake 375

notes: To the above recipe-tripled- add 6 oz choc chips-tripled recipe makes 88 cookies (29 cents)...is that 29 cents more...grand total of 60 cents...what year is this?!

Sesame Seed Cookies (Mary Carboni)

Beat 3 eggs with 1¼ c sugar and ½ tsp salt-Add 1 cup oil-Beat together-add 1 tsp vanilla and 1 tsp orange or lemon flavor-2½ tsps b. powder-3½ cups flour (maybe more)-shape-brush with egg wash(beat egg well) and then put on sesame seeds with fingers **(I guess she means sprinkle with sesame seeds)**

She notes: try baking at 365 degrees-bake 12 minutes-5 min lower shelf (2nd notch)-7 min on 4th notch-use shiny pans

Josie's Recipe Collection:

Cuchidati

Filling: 2 (14 or 15 oz) strings of figs-chopped fine
1 or 2 boxes seeded raisins
2 cups walnuts coarsely chopped (by hand)
1 cup sliced almonds toasted at 350 degrees for 2 min. - watch carefully-just until they
turn tan-crumble by hand
2 bars sweet choc chopped (in grinder) or 12 oz pkg <u>mini</u> choc chips (can use more)
peel from 1½ tangerines-chopped fine
8 oz honey-8 oz strawberry jam-1 10 oz bottle maraschino cherries (drained & chopped)
about 1¾ tsp cinnamon (2 tsps)
½ tsp black pepper-Mix thoroughly

notes: before grinding figs soak in warm water until they soften, drain, cut off stem & put thru grinder with raisins-tangerine peel & cherries-cut figs in two-go thru grinder better whiskey may be added to filling, I never did (color me surprised!)
In 1996 I used 2 boxes of raisins-mini chips are better because they don't have to be ground-choc bar is too hard to grind-lge choc chips are too hard to grind

My note...when I made these in 2002 I did not use cinnamon or black pepper I forgot them...and used the mini chips...I have her grinder...Lucy gave it to me because she said I'd be making the cookies

Pastry: 12 cups flour-1 cup granulated sugar-3 cups Crisco-1 tsp salt-24 tsps b. powder-2 tsps vanilla-about ½ cups cold water

Mix as you would pie pastry-Roll pastry-fill-shape & cut-bake in 375 degree oven-about 15 min-

Note: Use shiny pans-I bake cookies about 7 min on bottom rack and 7 or 8 min on top rack-

1996-8 cookie sheets -took 3 hrs to shape-2½ hrs to bake-3 hrs to frost-I forgot the cinnamon and black pepper

My note: 2002 I forgot the vanilla in the pastry and didn't notice a difference. Baked them on my baking stone at mid level in the oven for 15 to 20 min... Take the ground mixture and then add the nuts, cherries, honey and chocolate chips. Cutting and shaping these is very difficult. We rolled out small pieces of pastry...filled the center and folded the sides of the dough over and cut on diagonal.

Frosting: confectioner's sugar-vanilla & milk-Sprinkle with paparina (non pareils)

My note: These were Josie's Christmas specialty. Christmas 2002 Kimmy Ann visited in Florida and we made these together. I used butter in the frosting and decorated them with multi colored soft ice cream toppers. Kimmy Ann had a stroke "Little dots!! Grandma used little dots...these aren't little dots!" And the frosting was wrong she said because I used butter. She had spent a Christmas in New York and personally assisted her grandmother. Grandma brushed on white icing and I spooned on the frosting on the warm cookies...she had a fit!!

Éclairs (Lucy's)

1 pkg Vanilla pudding & pie filling
1½ cups milk
½ cup prepared dream whip-whipped topping
6 Tbsps butter or margarine
¾ cup water
¾ cup sifted all purpose flour
3 eggs
2 squares unsweetened chocolate
2 Tbsps butter
1½ cups un-sifted xxxx sugar
dash salt
3 Tbsps milk

<u>Filling</u>: Cook pudding as directed on package, reducing milk to 1½ cups-Cover surface with wax paper-chill 1 hour-Beat pudding until smooth-fold in prepared topping

<u>Shells</u>: Bring 6 Tbsps butter & the water to a boil in saucepan-Reduce heat rapidly stir in flour-Cook & stir until mixture leaves sides of pan (about 2 minutes)-Remove from heat-beat in eggs one at a time-Beat thoroughly until satiny-Form 5 x 1" strips of dough with spoon on ungreased cookie sheet-Bake 350 degrees for 30 min-Cool

<u>Glaze</u>: Melt choc with butter over low heat-Remove from heat-blend in sugar, salt & 3 Toss milk-Spread immediately on filled éclairs...makes 10

Almond Paste Cookies (Mary Feola's)

1½ # almond paste (on grater)-3 cups xxxx sugar-5 egg whites beaten stiff-grease & flour tins lightly-drop by tsps-let remain on pan 10 min-Bake at 325 degrees for 20 min-Cool in pan before removing

Mary was my mother's maid of honor and my beloved godmother

Cooked Almond Paste

2 eggs-¾ c superfine sugar-powdered sugar sifted-½ tsp vanilla-3 cups ground almonds-1 tsp lemon juice-Beat eggs until smooth in top of double boiler-stir in superfine sugar and 1¼ and 1¼ c xxxx sugar-Heat over simmering water-beating until thick & creamy-Remove from heat-Add almonds-vanilla & lemon juice-Mix to paste-Knead until smooth on board, lightly dusted with more xxxx sugar

****

Almond Paste

1½ c whole blanched almonds-1½ c sifted xxxx sugar-1 egg white-1 tsp almond flavoring-¼ tsp salt
Grind almonds in food processor or a portion at a time in electric blender-Combine with xxxx sugar, egg white-almond flavoring and salt-Knead to stiff paste-Makes about 1⅓ cups-Will keep months in refrigerator if wrapped tightly in plastic wrap or air tight container
My note: these last two recipes are for almond paste that is used in the Almond Paste Cookie recipes...I don't know what the term "grater" means in the cookie recipes...does this stuff have to be grated...never made almond cookies

Cherry Bon Bons (Rose B.) rose colored cookies

2 cups flour-1 tsp b. powder-1 3oz pkg cherry jello-2 3½ oz instant pudding-4 eggs separated-6 Tbsps milk-1 tsp almond extract-½ cup chopped walnuts-1½ cups flaked coconut-4 cups flaked coconut (to roll cookies)-2 tsps water-¾ cup to 1 cup oil
Mix well flour-b. powder-jello-pudding-add 4 egg yolks-oil-milk and almond extract-mix well-stir in walnuts and 1½ cups flaked coconut-Blend well-roll into balls about the size of a walnut (or smaller)-Beat egg whites with water-just to mix-Roll ball in egg white then in coconut-Bake on un-greased cookie sheet-Flatten slightly-Bake 12 to 15 min at 325 degrees (about 6 min on each rack)
She notes: I grease the cookie sheets lightly

For yellow cookies use vanilla instant pudding & orange jello/with orange or lemon extract
For green cookies use pistachio instant pudding & lime jello/with almond extract
For choc cookies use chocolate instant pudding & cherry jello/vanilla extract
Makes about 50 cookies

Mexican hats (Ponzarotta) Jo Barberio Cortez

6 cups flour   pinch of salt
1¼ cups Spry   3 eggs
enough warm water to make a soft dough
3½ tsps b. powder
Mix flour-b. powder-salt & Spry as you would for pie crust-
Add beaten eggs-Work into flour mixture and add warm
water-Knead dough until smooth-Cut into four pieces-let
stand 15 min.

Filling

2 # blanched, ground almonds-Brown in heavy skillet-keep
adding 1 cup sugar a little at a time-when almonds are browned
add a few drops of orange juice and rind of an orange-add
enough honey to hold together
Roll the dough-Cut with a small round cookie or donut cutter-
Fill one round with almond filling, just in center-Place another
cookie round over filling-Cut edges-fold every other one-Fry
in deep fat
**The cutting and folding directions are not clear to me...every
other one...how?...I picture sealing like a round ravioli**

Holiday Unbeatables

2 cups xxxx sugar-½ c flour-½ tsp b. powder-½ c egg whites-
2 cups chopped walnuts- 1 cup chopped candied cherries
In mixing bowl-combine sugar- flour- b. powder & egg whites-
Stir until thoroughly blended. Add walnuts & cherries-mix
well-drop by teaspoonfuls 2″ apart onto greased & floured
cookie sheets. Bake at 325 degrees 12 to 15 minutes. Let stand
2 to 3 min-remove from cookie sheets

Variations:
Substitute 2 cups chopped macadamia nuts-1 cup flaked
coconut-½ cup chopped candied pineapple for walnuts &
cherries
Substitute 1½ cup diced toasted almonds and 1½ cups after
dinner mints for walnuts & cherries
Substitute 2 cups chopped nuts & 1 cup chopped dates for the
walnuts & cherries

Chocolate Unbeatables: 2 cups xxxx sugar-½ tsp b. powder-
¼ c cocoa-½ c egg whites-2 c chopped walnuts-1 c flaked
coconut

**Notes: well greased and floured cookie sheets-yield about
48...farther down the page she writes to bake 10-15 min
instead of 12 to 15**

Cannoli Filling

I asked Mom for this recipe in the 1980's found the recipe card stuck in my cookbook

¾ cup sugar-3 Tbsps cornstarch-¾ cup milk-1 # ricotta-1½ tsp vanilla-½ cup semi sweet chocolate chips coarsely chopped

Combine sugar and cornstarch in a saucepan. Slowly stir in milk. Cook until thick and bubbly-stirring constantly. Cover surface with wax paper. Cool without stirring. With electric mixer beat ricotta until creamy. Blend in cornstarch mixture & vanilla. Stir in chocolate chip pieces.
She writes: This tastes just like filling in cannoli's from the café. Also makes a good filling between layers of sponge or angel food cake.

Toll House Marble Squares

Beat until creamy: ½ cup soft oleo-6 Tbsps sugar-6 Tbsps brown sugar-½ tsp vanilla-¼ tsp water. Beat in 1 egg. Sift-mix in 1 cup plus 2 Tbsps sifted flour-½ tsp b. soda-½ tsp salt-add ½ cup chopped walnuts-Spread in greased 13 x 9 x2" pan-Sprinkle with one 6 oz pkg choc chips-bake at 375 degrees for 1 minute-Run knife thru dough to marbleize-Bake 12 to 14 min more (24 squares)

Biscotti **(Florentine Café)**

3 eggs-¾ c sugar-¾ cup oil-3 cup flour-3 heaping tsps baking powder-1 tsp salt-1 tsp vanilla-½ small package almonds ground

Beat eggs-add sugar & oil, beat well-add vanilla-Sift flour with baking powder & salt-Add to liquids & mix well-Mix on board-if too soft add a little flour-dough should be on the soft side-Shape into 3 loaves on flat side–Let rise. Grease cookie sheet-Bake 350 degrees for 15 minutes. Let cool about 10 minutes-Slice-place cut side down on cookie sheet & toast for 5-6 minutes on each side or until brown-Cool on baking sheet

Florentine Cafe(makes 16)
Better known as pusties or posta shots

Filling: mix 1 cup sugar & 3 heaping Tbsps flour in a saucepan-
Add 2 cups milk-2 egg yolks-2 squares chocolate (or 4 Tbsps
cocoa)-Cook until thick stir in 1 tsps vanilla

Crust: mix 4 cups flour-2 cups brown sugar-1 tsp baking
powder in large bowl-Cut in 1 cup Crisco-add 2 eggs & 1 Tbsp
water-Mix-Take small balls of dough and press into tins-Fill
each with 2 Tbsps filling-Roll or press circles of dough for
tops-cover tarts flat-swish with egg white
Bake at 400 degrees for about 20 minutes until browned-*do
not put on cookie sheet -turn baked tarts on towel to cool –
remove tins and eat!!

***Do not put tart tins on a cookie sheet-place and bake
directly on oven rack**

**the previous 2 recipes are from the Florentine Café ...my
girlfriend gave them to me in 2003...Mom never saw these
recipes but I know she would have been thrilled to have
them**

**The late Dr. Arthur Petronio's grandparent's opened the
Florentine Café on Bleeker Street in Utica, New York. His
wife who I worked with in Faxton in the late 70's early 80's
and remains my dear friend passed these on to me. Her
husband's grandparents originally opened the café in the
early 1900's.**

Chocolate Cookies

(my mother referred to these as the chocolate/pepper cookies)

Makes about 4 doz-2½ " cookies

½ c shortening
1 c brown sugar (packed)   } mix these 4 items thoroughly
½ c granulated sugar
2 eggs

add 2 squares unsweetened chocolate –melted
Stir in: 1 cup cultured sour cream or undiluted evaporated milk & 1 tsp vanilla
Sift together and stir in: 2¾ c sifted flour-½ tsp baking soda-1 tsp salt-1 tsp cinnamon-½ tsp ground cloves-1 tsp allspice ½ tsp black pepper
Chill dough-drop rounded teaspoonfuls about 2" apart on greased baking sheet-bake just until…when touched gently with finger almost no imprint remains-temp 375 about 8-10 minutes

Instead of baking chocolate-I use 3 Tbsps cocoa plus 1 Tbsp shortening for each square of chocolate…sift cocoa with other dry ingredients…chopped walnuts, raisins, chocolate chips, maraschino or candied cherries are optional

My mother most always made these with walnuts…began leaving out the raisins when her children complained about raisins in everything even chocolate cookies

Chocolate Rolls

My all time favorite...can still see Aunt Angie rolling these babies up...my fingers in the chocolate filling...thanks to my cousin Geri for finding this recipe as my mother did not have this one written anywhere

1 can of condensed milk
1 lg pkg chocolate chips
1 cup walnuts
melt chocolate in milk cool lukewarm

Dough
2 sticks oleo
6 eggs
1 cup sugar
3 tsp baking powder
1 Tbsp vanilla
5-6 c flour

cream oleo, sugar, beat in egg-add flour-Roll dough like pie crust, spread chocolate filling-sprinkle nuts-roll dough on wax paper, roll like jelly roll, wrap wax paper around dough -Bake 350 degrees 15-20 minutes

well this wax paper thing is a bit confusing...I am assuming she means use the wax paper to wrap the dough in a jelly roll like fashion...but not to actually bake the wax paper... don'tcha think!!

Josie's Recipe Collection:

Libby's Great Pumpkin Cookies

2 cups all-purpose flour
$1^{1/3}$ cups quick or old-fashioned oats
1 teaspoon baking soda
1 teaspoon ground cinnamon
$1/2$ teaspoon salt
1 cup (2 sticks) butter or margarine, softened
1 cup packed brown sugar
1 cup granulated sugar
1 cup LIBBY'S 100% Pure Pumpkin
1 large egg
1 teaspoon vanilla extract
1 package of orange and brown Halloween M-n-Ms.

PREHEAT oven to 350 F. Grease baking sheets.

COMBINE flour, oats, baking soda, cinnamon and salt in medium bowl. Beat butter, brown sugar and granulated sugar in large mixer bowl until light and fluffy. Add pumpkin, egg, and vanilla extract; mix well. Add flour mixture; mix well. Stir in nuts and raisins. Spoon cookie dough onto prepared baking sheet; spread into circle or oval. Repeat with remaining dough.

BAKE for 14 to 16 minutes or until cookies are firm and lightly browned. Cool on baking sheets for 2 minutes; remove to wire racks to cool completely.

NOTES

PASTA

Josie and her mother Lucy Sgroi in the early 1940's

Basic Pasta

2½ c flour-2 egg whites-1 whole egg-¼ c water

In large bowl place 2 c flour. Combine egg whites & whole eggs & water. Add to flour and mix well. Sprinkle kneading surface with remaining flour. Turn dough out & knead 8 to 10 min. or until smooth & elastic. Cover-let rest 10 min. Divide dough into ⅓'s on lightly floured surface, roll each piece to a rectangle 15x12. If dough becomes to elastic during rolling, cover & let rest 5 min. Using sharp knife cut dough into strips of desired width.
Or dust surface of dough generously with flour & roll like a jelly roll–cut. Lift & shake noodles to separate. Cook fresh pasta in large amount of boiling water for 5 min. Drain-top with sauce or butter-do not rinse. Store pasta in plastic-refrigerate & use within 2-3 days.

Add oil to boiling water, is her note. I remember Aunt Angie leaving the pasta strips on floured dish towels to dry for a few hours. I got very good at removing the uncooked pasta and eating the raw dough...and moving the other strips around to make it look like nothing was missing... she wondered why I was too full to eat my dinner.

No mention of salt in recipe or water...need salt in water .

She has another page of the same recipe where she says to dry noodles at least 1 hour.

Noodles (1 portion)

1 c un-sifted flour-1 egg

Mix egg in flour with fingertips or fork. Dough will be very stiff, but after kneading 15 minutes-it will be more pliable (Bubbles will form) Roll it into a ball and leave for 20 minutes on a lightly floured board. Cover with bowl or cloth. Roll out even-paper thin. Dry 30 min. & cut.

Florence Valente's Cavatelli

6 c flour-3 Tbsps Spry-mix like pie dough
Add 2 cups boiling water-mix with wooden spoon-Knead until smooth-Cut dough in small pieces-roll like a cigar. (Sprinkle pan with flour to put cavatelli in as they come off machine)

Flour is needed to prevent sticking when frozen...she notes. I guess you need to know what to do with a cavatelli making machine to finish this recipe.

Baked Ziti

1 # browned hamburg-1 # ricotta-Romano cheese-¼ # mozzarella-parsley- 2eggs salt & pepper to taste
not a beginners cookbook...I guess you have to know you need a couple pounds of ziti and sauce...she forgot the sauce!

Filling for Baked Ziti or Baked Lasagna

More accurately titled...filling...slight revision

2 # ricotta-(about) 8 oz mozzarella-3 eggs-parsley chopped-salt & pepper-Romano or Parmesan cheese-Bake 350 degrees covered 10-15 min and then uncovered 20-30 min

she has "3 eggs" circled and has noted...more eggs. I always put in at least 2 per pound of ricotta. Baker's choice I guess.

Filling for Jumbo Shells

1 pkg shells
1 # ricotta
2 eggs
4 oz mozzarella
about ½ cup or more Parmesan cheese
little salt & pepper
parsley

that's it...do what you want with it

Manicotti (Mary Lazzuri)

6 eggs beaten well-1 cup milk-1½ c flour-½ tsp salt
Bake in 8" skillet-flip

Filling-2-2½ # ricotta-8 oz mozzarella grated-2 eggs-Parmesan cheese (at least 4 Tbsps)-blk. Pepper-very little salt-fresh parsley (optional)-milk if needed

Bake in single layer-spread sauce in pan-put in manicotti shells- spread more sauce on top-Spread shredded mozzarella over top.
Bake at 350 degrees (400 degrees) for ½ hr to 45 min

This note in the margin: spread filling on "pancakes"...roll & place on sauce in pan. I guess the eggs, milk, flour, and salt that has "flip" as directions...is the recipe for the dough. Make pasta rounds...like for cannelloni...fill and roll as she directs.

Uncooked Manicotti

Pour hot sauce in bottom of baking dish. Fill manicotti and arrange in pan in a single layer. Cover with more hot sauce-cover baking dish with aluminum foil-crimp edges for tight seal-Place in preheated 350 degree-Bake for 40 min-uncover-sprinkle with cheese-bake 10 more min-Serve hot

She neglects to say that the uncooked manicotti shells-right from the box- are filled with the cheese filling of your choice...just in case there is a novice reading this book. As I recall the shell cooked up a little gummy...and this recipe needs a great deal of sauce.

Sausage Stuffed Shells

1 pkg jumbo shells (need 36 unbroken)
12 oz mozzarella-1 # gr. beef-½ # sweet sausage, loose and out of casing-⅔ cup fresh white bread crumbs-3 Tbsps parsley-salt & pepper-⅓ c milk-1 lge egg-4 cups tomato sauce
Fry gr. beef & sausage-drain-mix with br. crumbs-parsley-salt & pepper-milk-eggs and ½ of the mozzarella (grated).
1 heaping Tbsp filling for each shell
Put sauce in bottom of pan-place shells in pan pour more sauce over shells & the remaining mozzarella over the top of shells-350 degrees-30 min.
Let stand 15 min. before serving-To make ahead-prepare as directed-do not bake-freeze-Before baking-thaw in refrig over night-Bake covered at 350 degrees-45 min. or until heated thru'

Cavatelli

6 cups flour-3 Tbsps shortening-1½ cups hot water-sift flour & form a well. Place hot water and melted shortening inside of well-blend thoroughly and knead until smooth

Rita's Cavatelli

2 # ricotta-2 # flour-2 eggs

Florence Maneen Valente's Cavatelli

2 # ricotta-1 # flour

Potato Cavatelli

6 cups flour-3 boiled potatoes-2 Tbsps oil or shortening-1 egg

short and sweet...you have to know how to make cavatelli to utilize these recipes...this is a second Florence Valente's cavatelli

Ravioli Dough (Sammy's graduation)

8 c flour-1 tsp salt-5 eggs plus 1¼ to 1½ cups water
(makes 100 small & about 30 to 35 large

the filling for above
2 # ricotta-8 oz mozzarella-3 eggs-parsley-salt & pepper to taste.
Flour ravioli plates generously-cook in boiling water about 10 min

She made her own for my brother Sammy's high school graduation party

I have found over the years that steaming frozen ravioli in a large frying pan maintains the integrity of the pasta...they don't break and lose cheese stuffing...that's my tip...sorry I never made my own!

Manicotti

4 eggs-¼ cup water-¾ c un-sifted flour (fork stir to aerate before measuring) ¼ tsp salt

Mary Sylvester: 2 c water-2 eggs-2 cups flour

Beat all ingredients together. Place a skillet with rounded bottom (8" across top-6-6½ across bottom) over low heat. For each pancake lightly brush skillet with melted butter or oil. Pour batter from a ¼ measuring cup filled a little over half full (2½ Tbsps) into hot greased skillet-lifting and rotating pan as you pour-in order to spread batter over entire bottom of pan. If batter is too thick-stir in a little water. Cook over low heat just to set-about 20 seconds. Turn & cook to set other side. They will not be brown. As they cook-stack them on a plate (10 to 12)

Cheese filling-1 # ricotta-½ tsp salt-4 oz mozzarella-¼ cup Parmesan cheese-¼ tsp pepper-1 tsp minced parsley-1 egg-Beat together
Spread ¼ cup cheese filling down center of each pancake-roll up and place in 2 qt oblong glass dish (11¾ x 7½ x 1¾) Pour tomato sauce over pancakes. Sprinkle with extra Parmesan cheese. Bake in preheated 350 degree oven until bubbly hot-40 to 45 min. Makes 5 to 6 servings-2 pancakes per person (?)

Well there you go...directions for manicotti

Baked Ziti (2#)

Sauce: 2 lge cans tomato puree-½ of 1 can tomato paste-put in kettle-place on stove-let simmer about 1 hr. In small sauté pan-little oil in pan (about 2 Tbsp) heat a little-add ½ med onion diced-1 clove garlic diced-chopped parsley-chopped basil (Fresh better-or dried) stir-when onion is translucent (do not brown) add to sauce pot-let simmer about 1 hr.

Filling: Add about 3 cups of sauce to 1 # gr beef and 1 # sausage (remove from casing) which has been browned-drain oil from meat-add to the 3 cups of sauce-heat together for a few min.

To the remaining sauce in pot add any of the following or a combination of any of the following: br. meatballs-br. sausage-br. pork-br. spare ribs. Use for extra sauce for any pasta dish.

Easy Tomato Sauce

Dilute 2 6oz cans tomato paste with 3 cans of water in a small saucepan-Stir in ½ tsp crushed leaf basil and ½ tsp crushed leaf oregano-1 crushed garlic clove-2 tsps brown sugar-½ tsp salt and ¼ tsp black pepper. Heat 10 min-refrigerate-Makes 3½ cups sauce
Note: Use this for making young Mrs. B's eggplant recipe

Lasagna

2 # Lasagna pasta noodles
1 # mozzarella
2 # ricotta
½ cup Romano cheese
1½ # browned sausage

8-10 eggs beaten
¼ tsp blk pepper
½ tsp salt
½ tsp parsley
1½ # browned
hamburg

2 qts tomato puree & tomatoes cooked down; mix thoroughly-beaten eggs-ricotta-grated cheese-salt-pepper & parsley; Layer lasagna noodles in pan-then ricotta mixture-grated mozzarella-meat & sauce until pan is almost full.
Bake until heated thru' & bubbly @350 degrees

Meat Filling for 1# Manicotti Shells

1 # ground beef
½ # ground pork…or 1½ # gr. beef
1 egg
½ # grated mozzarella
½ c grated cheese
¾ c milk
3 slices bread
1 Tbsp chopped parsley
salt & pepper to taste

Soak bread in milk-sauté meat in oil-Blend meat, bread & milk, grated cheese with egg and parsley, salt & pepper-place sauce in pan-single layer stuffed manicotti 350 degrees

This note in margin: check this out-16 shells; Gioia shells thinner than P&R

This fills 23 shells:
2 # hamburg browned
1½ c shredded mozzarella
6 Tbps grated cheese
½ c seasoned bread crumbs
parsley & pepper & salt
2 eggs slightly beaten-plus water

Tomato Sauce

¼ cup oil-1 onion minced-1 clove garlic minced-1 small pepper diced-Basil-parsley-salt. Sauté the above-add 2 cans (29 oz) tomato sauce or crushed tomatoes-1 can tomato paste-2 tsp sugar-water-cook over low heat partially covered about 1½ hrs.

ENTREES

Girlfriends and their mothers

Potato Filling

(fills empty stomachs)

Serves 4-6-bake at 350 degrees-1 hour-Preheat oven to 350 degrees

Sauté in skillet ¼ c oleo-1 c chopped celery-1 c chopped onions

Pare & boil in salted water-4 med sized potatoes-when done mash

Into potatoes mix 1 egg slightly beaten-2 slices bread torn into small pieces-onions & celery-Season with salt & pepper to taste-Put into greased baking dish-Bake for 1 hour-Cover for first half hour-uncover for remaining time

Baked Beans (Mrs. Bennison's)

Campbell's pork & beans-Worcestershire sauce-prepared mustard-catsup-sliced onion-molasses or brown sugar on top-bacon-Bake at 350 degrees until bubbly

I guess you can prepare as you wish...throw in as much of the ingredients as you like.

Cheese Potatoes

6 med potatoes, cooked and skinned-¼ c butter-2 cups shredded cheddar cheese-1 tsp salt-1½ c sour cream at room temp-¼ tsp pepper-½ c chopped onion-2 Tbsps butter
Cool potatoes & shred coarsely-combine cheese and butter over low heat until melted-Remove from heat & blend in cream-onions-salt & pepper. Fold in potatoes & put in greased 2 qt casserole-Dot with butter-Bake 25 min at 350 degrees

Aunt Mary gave me her cheat version...butter a 2 qt casserole-throw in raw potatoes-onion-salt & pepper-diced ham if you prefer and cover with Campbell's cheddar soup...1 can blended with ½ can milk...bake covered and uncovered for last 15 min.

Minestrone

1 small onion minced-1 garlic clove minced-2 Tbsps oil-1 c chopped tomatoes-¾ c diced celery-5 beef bouillon cubes-1 cup chopped cabbage or broccoli-1 tsp salt-⅛ tsp pepper-1 # can of beans-1 cup cooked macaroni-¼ c grated Parmesan cheese

Potatoes (oven fried)

Cut pared potatoes lengthwise into strips about ½" wide-Soak in cold water about 20 min-Drain thoroughly-Place in shallow baking dish or pan containing ¼ to ½" melted Crisco-Place in hot oven-450 degrees-Turn occasionally-Allow about 35 to 40 min for potatoes to brown and cook through.

Baked Butter Beans

2 med cans large butter beans-1 Tbsp mustard-1 med onion chopped-½ cup catsup-½ # bacon cut up-1 cup dark brown sugar-Partially cook bacon-drain off fat-Drain liquid off bean-Mix all ingredients-Bake at 300 degrees for 2 hours

Broccoli Rice Bake

2 c cooked rice-1 pkg chopped broccoli cooked and drained-1 8oz jar cheese whiz-1 can mushroom soup-¼ c chopped celery-¼ c chopped onion-Mix and bake at 350 degrees-1 hour

Notes in margin: I didn't have cheese whiz-I used 4 slices of cheese broken in pcs-Instead of mushroom soup I used chicken soup and sliced mushrooms drained.
Is that cream of chicken?...I'm guessing.

Deviled Ham Zucchini Bake (Toaster oven)

2 cups sliced zucchini ¼" thick-1 4oz can mushrooms sliced & drained-1 4oz bottle sliced ripe olives drained-1 cup (4oz) shredded cheese-5 eggs-⅓ cup milk-2 Tbsps flour-1 4½ oz can deviled ham-3 tsps instant minced onion-⅛ tsps instant minced garlic-2 Tbsps pimento
In a 1½ qt shallow baking pan layer zucchini-mushrooms-olives & cheese. In a bowl beat together eggs-milk-ham-flour-onion & garlic. Pour over zucchini. Top with pimento-Bake in toaster oven T 350 degrees (6 servings)

Another zucchini recipe I didn't eat...she loved the stuff.

Mixed Baked Veg

4 med boiling potatoes-3 sweet red or green peppers-3 ripe
tomatoes-4 med onions-1 Tbsp salt-Freshly ground pepper
Pare potatoes-cut in 8ths-Quarter & seed peppers-Cut
tomatoes in 6ths-Peel onions-quarter peppers-Cut tomatoes
in 6ths-Peel onions & quarter-Fit veg in 13 x 9 x 2" pan-add
oil, salt & pepper-Bake 400 degree oven 45 min-stirring every
15 min until potatoes are tender-if there is a lot of liquid at the
end of baking time-turn oven to 450 degrees until most liquid
evaporates.

**Well here's an exact recipe...even tells us in how many
pieces to cut the veggies.**

Zucchini Rounds

⅓ c biscuit mix-¼ c cheese (Romano)-⅛ tsp pepper-2 eggs
slightly beaten-2 cups shredded zucchini-2 Tbsps butter
Use 2 Tbsps mixture for each round-Cook 4 rounds at a time-
2 to 3 minutes each-Makes 12 rounds
Notes: add more Bisquik-try baking instead of frying

Josie's Recipe Collection:

Stuffed Onions

4 onions (med)

2 Tbsps oil-2 Tbsps Balsamic vinegar-¼ c fresh parsley-¼ c bread crumbs-¼ c grated Parmesan cheese-¼ tsp salt-¼ tsp pepper-⅛ tsp Italian seasoning
Preheat oven to 350 degrees-cut onions crosswise-trim ends so they'll stay flat-Scoop out centers with melon baller & reserve-Pour 1 Tbsp oil in baking dish-Add onions, turning to coat-Arrange cut side up-Drizzle with vinegar-Cover dish with foil-Bake 45 min or until tender-Mince reserved onion centers-Transfer to small bowl-Stir in remaining oil-parsley-bread crumbs-cheese-salt & pepper & Italian seasoning-Mound mixture evenly in center of each onion half & bake uncovered 20 min or until tender
Notes: optional-add lightly br. hamburg or partially cooked sausage

Mousaka

Eggplant or zucchini

1½ # potatoes-Fat for frying-2 med onions chopped-¼ c oil-1 # hamburg-2 cloves garlic-1 8oz can tomato sauce-1 tsp cinnamon-salt & pepper-2 eggs-1 c milk-⅓ c grated cheese
Pan fry potatoes, eggplant or zucchini-Drain-arrange ½ in an even layer-Saute onion, set aside-In remaining oil cook beef-add cinnamon- garlic-tom. sauce-onion-salt & pepper-Pour over eggplant or zucchini & potatoes-Do second layer-Beat eggs & milk-Pour over-sprinkle with cheese-375 degree oven-45 minutes

Well I could use a few hints here...is this potatoes and zucchini, potatoes and eggplant...or...potatoes or eggplant or zucchini...after reading it a couple of times...it seems as though it is the combo of potato and veggie

Golden Crumb Broccoli Casserole

1½ lbs fresh broccoli (cut up) 6 cups-1 can condensed cream of mushroom soup-¼ c mayonnaise-¼ cup (1oz) shredded Am. Cheese-1 Tbsp chopped pimento-1½ tsp lemon juice-½ cup rich round cheese cracker crumbs (6 crackers)
Cook broccoli in small amt of boiling salted water 10 to 15 min & drain-Turn into 1½ qt casserole-Combine soup-mayonnaise-cheese-pimento and lemon juice. Pour over broccoli-Top with cracker crumbs. Bake in 350 degree oven for 35 min.
6 to 8 servings

Broccoli Casserole

Broccoli cuts-¼ c milk-1 can mushroom soup-1 slice of Am. Cheese-1 egg-2 Tbsps mayonnaise-Bake 1 hr. Sprinkle gently with buttered bread crumbs and Italian cheese.

Combine as you please and pick an oven temp!

Josie's Recipe Collection:

Eggplant Parmigiana Express

Mrs. B's recipe-young Mrs. B

1 med size eggplant (about 1½ #)-½ cup packaged breadcrumbs-¾ cup Parmesan cheese-¼ cup mayonnaise-1 pkg 8 oz mozzarella cheese, sliced-1 cup easy tomato sauce **(found at the end of the pasta section in this book)**
Wash & trim eggplant-cut into ½" slices. Combine crumbs and ¼ cup cheese on wax paper. Spread mayonnaise thinly on both sides of one eggplant slice, dip into crumb mixture coating both sides. Place on un-greased cookie sheet-repeat with remaining slices. Bake in hot oven 425 degrees **(she has a note above this temp- 412 degrees)** about 15 minutes or until fork tender & browned. Remove from oven-lower temp to 375 degrees-Grease a 11¾ x 1¾" baking pan & arrange eggplant slices, slightly overlapping. Spread each slice with a small amount of tomato sauce. Cover with slices of mozzarella. Sprinkle with half of grated cheese-spoon remaining sauce over and sprinkle with remaining cheese. Bake at 375 degrees for 15 min or until cheese is melted-makes 4-6 servings

Celery & Eggplant Croquettes

½ med eggplant (½ #) peeled and minced-2 cups diced celery-½ cup diced onion-1½ cups bread crumbs dried-1 egg-1 tsp salt-oil
Cook eggplant-celery & onion in ½ cup boiling water, covered-10 minutes or until eggplant is tender-drain well. Stir in ½ c dried crumbs-egg & salt. Cover and refrigerate 15 minutes before serving. In electric skillet heat 1" salad oil to 375 degrees-Shape a heaping Tbsp vegetable mixture into a log 2" long-Roll in remaining bread crumbs-Makes 12 croquettes. Fry 3 or 4 at a time until golden brown-turn once-drain on paper towels. 3 per serving

Zucchini Squash Casserole

6 cups cooked zucchini squash-½ c chopped onion-1 cup sour cream-1 can cream of chicken soup-1 c shredded raw carrots-4 ozs sharp cheese, shredded-1 8oz pkg herb seasoned stuffing mix-½ cup melted butter
Cook and drain squash-Combine onion, soup, sour cream, carrots and cheese with squash-<u>Melt</u> butter and combine with stuffing mix-Spread ½ stuffing mix over bottom of 9" x 9" casserole dish-Pour squash mixture over this-Top with remaining stuffing mixture-Bake at 350 degrees for one hour (8 servings)

Steamed Clams

Wash & scrub in running water as many clams as will be required-removing all sand etc.-Place clams in upper perforated section of steamer-Place cold water, about one cup for each two quarts of clams, in bottom section-Assemble steamer with cover in place-Steam over moderate heat until shells half open
Season melted butter with lemon juice-salt & pepper-Remove clams from shells-dip in butter mixture and eat all except the neck
Season clam broth from lower section to taste & serve in bouillon cups

Tuna Rice Fritters

⅔ c uncooked rice-1 tsp salt-1½ c boiling water-1 7 oz can tuna fish drained-¼ c milk-2 eggs separated-2 Tbsps flour-⅛ tsp pepper-oil for frying-Put 1st 3 ingredients in saucepan-bring to a boil-cook covered 15 min.-Drain if necessary-Mix tuna, milk, egg yolks, flour & pepper-add to rice and mix well-Fold in stiffly beaten egg whites-Drop by Tbsps into deep hot fat (375 degrees) & fry until brown-Drain on absorbent towels (4 servings)

Chinese Rice

(Sister Mary Lazzuri & her sister Josephine)

1 cup rice-chicken breast cut in small pieces-1 can mushrooms-soy sauce to your liking-carrots-celery-onions-garlic
Sauté each ingredient separately-sauté rice in oil-add soy sauce-add hot water with chicken bouillon-Add seasoning to taste-salt & pepper

Notes: also chicken gravy; and a ? by garlic; no cooking time...sounds like a skillet recipe to me.

Salmon Loaf (4 servings)

1 # can salmon (reserve ¼ c liquid)-1 tsp lemon rind-½ c chopped onion-2 Tbsps lemon juice-1½ c soft bread crumbs-⅛ tsp Tabasco sauce-1 tsp sugar-⅛ tsp pepper-2 eggs slightly beaten-¼ c chopped green pepper
Flake salmon-combine with other ingredients-Moisten with salmon liquid-Spoon into oiled quart loaf pan-Bake in 350 degree oven-35 to 40 min-Garnish with lemon slices

Salmon Croquettes

1 can of salmon-1 c soft bread crumbs-1 Tbsp minced onion-1 Tbsp chopped parsley-1 tsp lemon juice-⅛ tsp pepper-½ tsp salt-1 egg, beaten-1 Tbsp melted Crisco
Bone fish-Stir in bread crumbs-add egg, seasoning & Crisco-Mix & shape into croquettes-Roll in fine dry bread crumbs (additional)-Deep fry until golden brown-Recipe doubled makes 15 croquettes
Serve with chili sauce in little lemon cups for attractiveness

Tuna Treat

Prepare a pkg of brown & serve French bread-split-toast. Mix 1 can cream of celery or mushroom soup-7 oz can tuna drained & flaked-2 chopped hard cooked eggs-1 Tbsp chopped pimento. Spread mixture evenly over bread surfaces-cover edges completely-Broil about 4" from heat or until hot and bubbly. Top with 2 sliced hard boiled eggs-2 Tbsps parsley chopped. (6 to 8 servings)

Need 4 hard boiled eggs.

Rice Crusted Tuna Pie

⅔ cooked rice-1½ Tbsp melted oleo-3 eggs-2 tomatoes-French dressing-1 can solid packed tuna-¾ c scalded milk-1¾ c finely grated Swiss cheese-¼ tsp salt-⅛ tsp pepper-snipped scallions

In a bowl combine rice-oleo and slightly beaten egg (1)-Turn rice mixture into 9" pie plate-Using back of tablespoon press it firmly against sides and bottom of pie plate-Keep mixture high on rim of plate-Cut tomatoes in wedges (6) & let stand in French dressing to cover-Flake tuna-sprinkle ¾ grated cheese over pie crust-top with half the tuna-then remaining cheese-piling it high in center-Combine until well blended, milk, 2 eggs, salt & pepper-Pour this mixture over cheese in rice lined pie plate-Sprinkle remaining tuna on top-Bake at 375 degrees-25 min-place tomato slices & scallions all around inner edge-return to oven and bake until knife comes out clean (8 servings)

Notes: oven temp changed to 375 degrees from 400 degrees... after placing tomato slices cook about 15 minutes more... sometimes more
She doesn't say but the rice is cooked in this recipe...she loved this recipe.

Josie's Recipe Collection:

Chicken Rice Dinner

1 cup rice-5 # chicken-2 carrots-1 pt tomatoes or stock-⅛ tsp white pepper-1 tsp salt-2 onions-cut up fowl in pieces suitable for serving-Cover with boiling water-add rice-salt & pepper, chopped carrots, onions and tomatoes-Simmer in slow oven (350 degrees) for 2 or 3 hours-mushrooms may be substituted for carrots

I think I'd add mushrooms to this and use chicken & beef stock...my thought.

Turkey Breast

Heat oven to 350 degrees-In a 9 x 9" or 11 x 7" pan (shallow) place turkey breast roast-Pour 1 c orange juice over turkey-Sprinkle with tsp gr. sage-½ tsp thyme-½ tsp pepper-½ tsp salt-and 1 tsp orange peel-Baste occasionally for 1 hr & 30 to 35 min-Let stand 10 min before slicing (8 servings)

Good Dish for Brunch

8 slices bread trimmed & cubed **(best if stale but not rocky)**-1½ # link sausage cooked and sliced in small pieces-¾ # grated cheddar cheese-2¼ c whole milk (not skim)-1 14oz can drained mushrooms or fresh mushrooms-4 eggs (beaten a little)-1 can cream of mushroom soup-1½ tsps powdered mustard

Place cubed bread on bottom of long baking dish-Add cheese-layer sausage-then pour over this the mixture of milk-mushrooms-soup and eggs-mustard-Put in refrigerator overnite-Remove from refrig for 1 hr before baking-Bake 1 hr at 325 degrees

That's what the name of this dish is "good dish for brunch"

Stuffed Pork Shoulder (Bricioli)

Have butcher cut pork shoulder so you can stuff it-or use 3 slices boneless pork steak, layered shingle style
Stuffing-1 pkg frozen whole leaf spinach, squeeze out all water-spread over meat-add ½ c ricotta-¾ # It. sausage-2 hard boiled eggs chopped-1 sm. onion diced-all the above is layered on meat-Roll up with help of saran wrap-Tie with string that has been soaked in water-Bake about 1 ½ hrs
I'm guessing she pre cooked the sausage for this recipe... even though she didn't say...she did for all her other stuffed recipes...how many remember her using sewing thread instead of butcher's twine and having to eat some thread with Sunday dinner!

Fish Chowder

1 # fillets (haddock or cod)-2 med potatoes pared-2 Tbsps oleo or butter-1 med onion very thinly sliced-½ bay leaf-¼ tsp pepper-¼ tsp thyme-1¼ c boiling water-1 cup half & half-chopped parsley
Preheat oven to 375 degrees-Cut fish in 4 pieces-Place fish in a 12 x 8 x 2″ baking dish-add potatoes-onions-butter-bay leaf-salt & pepper & thyme-Pour water and half & half-Cover with foil-Bake 35 to 40 min or until potatoes are fork tender-Remove from oven-uncover-remove & discard bay leaf-Sprinkle with parsley, if desired.
Serves 4 **(88 cents each serving)**

Linda Young's Nite Before Christmas Breakfast

(Serves 6)

7 slices of bread-½ tsp salt-8 oz shredded cheddar cheese-¼ tsp pepper-6 eggs-3 cups milk-1 tsp dry mustard-3 strips bacon

The nite before Christmas cut bread into small cubes-In a lge bowl toss cheese & bread cubes together-Beat eggs & milk together-stir in salt & pepper & dry mustard-Pour this over bread and cheese in bowl-Mix thoroughly-Pour into a greased baking dish-Cut strips of raw bacon in half-arrange them on top of ingredients in baking dish-Cover dish with saran wrap & refrigerate overnite-In the A.M. remove from refrig-bake uncovered in preheated oven

Notes in margin: 350 degrees for 50-55 min-Bacon should be browned & crisp. Try a little lower oven temp 335 degrees. Baking dish-glass dish 7½ x 11½ "

So this is a breakfast for Christmas that you make the night before...not a night before Christmas meal...good thing because there is no meat on Christmas Eve!!

Chicken Delicious

6 med potatoes peeled & quartered-½ tsp pepper-1 tsp each paprika & oregano-1 frying chicken (cut up)-½ tsp garlic salt-1 # sweet or hot sausage (cut up)-⅓ cup vegetable oil
Arrange potatoes in large shallow 3 quart casserole-Mix seasonings and sprinkle some on potatoes-arrange chicken and sausage on top-Pour oil over mixture and sprinkle with remaining seasonings
Cover and bake in hot oven (425 degrees) 1 hour-Reduce heat to 375 degrees-uncover casserole and bake 30 min or longer until chicken and potatoes are well browned
Notes: Good with garlic bread and green salad 4-6 servings. I didn't have sausage I used 2 chickens.
I want to know if she told her cardiologist about this recipe... all that oil over sausage. I would have to revamp this recipe to the cooking light version before I could eat it.

Chicken Casserole

In bowl combine 2 c cooked rice-1½ c diced celery-2 c cooked diced chicken-1 c rich chicken broth-1 3 ½ oz can sliced mushrooms with liquid-½ c chopped green onions-⅛ tsp blk pepper
Turn mixture into 2 qt casserole-sprinkle with mixture of ½ c fine dry bread crumbs and ½ Tbsp melted oleo plus ½ c chopped pecans-Bake in preheated oven-350 degrees-45 min. until heated through

Ann Landers Meatloaf

2 # gr. round steak-2 eggs-1½ c bread crumbs-¾ c catsup-1 tsp accent-½ c warm water-1 pkg Lipton's onion soup mix
Beat thoroughly. Put into meat loaf pan-Cover with 2 strips of bacon-Pour over 1 8oz can Hunts tomato sauce-350 degrees-1 hr-6 servings

Josie's Recipe Collection:

Lipton Surprise Meatloaf

Preheat oven to 375 degrees-Combine 1 envelope Lipton Onion Soup mix-2 eggs slightly beaten-¼ cup catsup and ¾ cup warm water add 1½ to 2 cups soft bread crumbs and 2 # ground beef-Spread half of mixture in 9 x 5 x 3" loaf pan-Press hard cooked eggs lightly into center of meat mixture arranging end to end-Cover with remaining mixture-bake 1 hr. or until done. 6 to 8 servings

Lipton Mushroom Swiss Steak

2 # chuck or round steak, 1" thick-heavy duty foil-1 envelope Lipton Beef Flavored Mushroom soup mix-Preheat oven to 375 degrees
Place meat in foil and sprinkle both sides with mushroom mix-Wrap loosely in foil, sealing edges air tight with double fold-Place in shallow baking pans and bake for 1 hour or until fork tender-4 servings.

Lipton Chopped Beef Stroganoff

1½ # ground beef
1 envelope Onion Soup Mix
3 Tbsps flour
3T tomato paste
2½ c water
½ c sour cream

Brown meat-Blend in onion soup-flour & tomato paste-Stir in water-simmer covered 10 min.-Stir in sour cream-Serve on noodles-Garnish with parsley-4 to 6 servings

Pork Chops

2 pork chops **(thick ones)**-2 cloves crushed garlic rubbed on pork chops-salt & pepper-fennel seeds on chops-Pound into chops with plate-Turn chops & put fennel seeds etc on that side-heat pan-add oil-throw in chops-fry until brown-lower heat & let them cook

Not as well scripted as her other recipes....chop, chop... pound...throw ...fry.

Marinade for Lamb Chops

1 Tbsps fresh rosemary-¼ tsp sage-2 cloves crushed garlic-2 Tbsps oil-1 Tbsp lemon juice-Marinate chops 3 hrs-hot broiler-5 min on each side

Pot Roast with Vegetables (Brown in Bag)

3-4 lbs beef for pot roast	6 carrots pared
flour	1 envelope onion soup mix

6 small potatoes peeled or 2 large quartered
⅓ cup water

Shake 1 Tbsp flour in empty bag-Trim excess fat from meat-Rub roast with flour-Place bag in pan and sprinkle half of onion soup mix on bottom-Put roast in bag-arrange vegetables around roast-Sprinkle remaining onion soup mix over roast and vegetables-add water-Tie bag-puncture 6 ½ " slits in top-Cook in preheated 325 degree oven-2½-3 hours-Pierce with fork to test for doneness

Josie's Recipe Collection:

Oven Fried Chicken Parmesan (4 servings)

1 cup crushed packaged herb stuffing or coarse dry bread crumbs-⅔ c grated Parmesan cheese-¼ c chopped parsley-1 clove garlic minced-Combine stuffing crumbs, cheese, parsley & garlic-Dip chicken in butter-roll in crumbs-Place pieces skin side up so they do not touch, in jelly roll pan or shallow pan-Sprinkle with the remaining butter & crumbs-Bake in moderate oven-375 degrees-45 min or until tender (turning un-necessary)
Note: If using bread crumbs-add 2 tsps salt & dash pepper)

For Brunch Egg & Sausage Quiche

Pastry for 1 crust-8 oz bulk pork sausage-4 hard cooked eggs-1 cup (4 oz) Natural Swiss cheese (chopped)-3 beaten eggs-¼ c lite cream or milk-¾ tsp salt-⅛ tsp pepper-Line 9' pie plate with pastry-Flute edges-do not prick-Bake in 350 degree oven for 7 min-Cook sausage & drain well-Sprinkle hard cooked eggs on bottom of shell-Top with Swiss cheese-Combine beaten eggs, cream, salt & pepper-Pour over all-Bake in 350 degree oven 30-35 min or until set-Let stand 10 min before serving. Serves 6

Hey she forgot to add the sausage!!!...I guess you put the sausage on top of the hardboiled eggs...Josie forgot...so unlike her.

Antoinette's Bar B Qued Spare Ribs

Boil ribs for about 10 min-4 # spare ribs-Sprinkle with 1 tsp garlic salt-Put in a little water-Brown in 450 degree oven for 20 min
Make Sauce: Sauté ¼ cup chopped onion in 1 Tbsp oil-3 Tbsps Worcestershire sauce and grated rind of 1 lemon-2 Tbsps br. sugar-⅓ c lemon juice-¾ tsp salt-½ tsp ginger-1 c chili sauce-1 cup syrup from pineapple slices-Simmer together 5 min-Pour over ribs-Reduce heat to 325 degrees-Bake until tender-Baste often-
Very good-Realemon may be used for the fresh lemon juice

Chicken Breasts

3 large chicken breasts (skinned - boned, and halved lengthwise)
6 thin slices boiled ham
1 med tomato seeded and chopped
3 slices mozzarella cheese – halved
½ tsp dried sage crushed
⅓ cup fine dry bread crumbs
2 Tbsps grated Parmesan cheese
2 Tbsps butter or margarine-melted

Place chicken boned side up on cutting board. Place a piece of clear plastic wrap over; Working from the center out, pound lightly with meat mallet to 5x5 inches. Remove wrap. Place a ham slice and a half slice of cheese on each cutlet to fit. Top with some tomato and a dash of sage. Tuck in sides-roll up jelly- roll style, pressing to seal well. Combine bread crumbs, parmesan cheese and parsley. Dip chicken in butter then roll in crumbs. Place in shallow baking dish. Bake 350 degree oven 40 to 45 min Serves 6

Josie's Recipe Collection:

Gravy for Pot Roast

The gravy for pot roast maybe thickened with cornstarch. It brings out the good flavors of the meat as well as vegetables. For each cup of broth-stir together 1½ Tbsps cornstarch and 2 Tbsps cold water until smooth and then stir in broth. Cook over moderate heat, stirring constantly until clear, thickened and boiling.

Swiss Steak Brown in Bag

Round steak – ½ to ¾" thick
Cut into pieces
Dredge in ¼ cup flour
Place in single layer in pan
Add 1 cup water-8 oz sauce (or tomatoes)- seasonings
Punch 4 holes in bag-Let stand 10 min
Bake at 350 degrees 1 hr 15 min

cook precisely for 1 hour and 15 minutes...but only the word "seasonings"...and don't forget the 4 holes...not 5...but 4!!

London Broil

2½ # flank steak-⅓ oil-⅓ c garlic red wine vinegar
3 Tbsps finely chopped onion-1 Tbsp Worcestshire sauce
½ tsp salt-½ tsp thyme-⅛ tsp pepper-¼ c butter (melted)
2 Tbsps minced parsley

Place steak in glass baking dish, combine ⅓ c water and the next 7 ingredients- Cover and marinate in refrigerator 2 hours or overnite, turning once or twice-Remove meat from marinade-drain on paper towels. Preheat broiler-Broil 3" from heat-3 minutes on each side; Cut in thin slices across grain diagonally. Pour butter over-cut steak-Garnish with parsley. Serve with broiled mushrooms, spinach & garlic bread.

Un-stuffed Pork Chops

(omit apple Little Sammy doesn't like it)
Brown 5 or 6 pork chops (about ½" thick) evenly on top of range. Set aside. Combine ¼ c butter (½ stick) and 1½ c water -bring to boiling
Add 1 (8 oz) pkg (about 5½ c) stuffing mix and 1 cup coarsely chopped unpeeled apple. Toss gently till moisture is absorbed
Spoon stuffing into lightly greased 9" square baking pan
Arrange chops over stuffing
Cover pan. Bake at 350 degrees-30minutes, remove cover, bake 10 min. more

I bet Sammy would eat it now!

Chicken & Stuffing Casserole

Place 2 cups sliced cooked chicken or turkey in greased 1½ qt. Casserole. Drain 1 (4oz) can mushrooms **(stems & pieces)** reserving fluid
Top chicken with mushrooms and ½ (8 oz) pkg of stuffing (2¾ c)
Combine mushroom liquid with 1-10½ oz can cream of chicken soup. Blend in enough hot water to make 2 cups. Pour over stuffing-Bake at 325 degrees. 40 to 45 min. 4 to 5 servings

Chicken Casserole

3 c cooked chicken or turkey-⅓ c sliced green onions-4½ oz sliced mushrooms, drained-¼ to ½ tsp slat-1cup shredded Swiss cheese (4 oz)-1½ c milk-¾ Bisquick-3 eggs

400 degree oven-Lightly grease 10" pie pan-Sprinkle turkey or chicken - mushrooms-onions-salt & cheese on plate. Beat remaining ingredients until smooth-one minute with beater. Pour into pie plate. Bake until golden brown and when knife is inserted ½ way between center & edge comes out clean-30 to 35 min. Let stand 5 min before cutting. Garnish with parsley-Refrigerate leftovers. 6-8 servings

Italian Meatloaf

Meatball mixture (1 # hamburg)
½ cup grated Parmesan cheese

1 or 2 eggs	small clove minced garlic
½ cup dried bread crumbs	chopped parsley
2 or 3 Tbsps water	salt & pepper

In a large bowl beat eggs, add water (to moisten bread crumbs) salt-pepper, garlic & parsley. Let stand a few minutes-then add cheese & hamburg & mix thoroughly. Pat on a sheet of plastic wrap. **(rectangle about ___ x___ inches)**
Filling: about 6 slices of boiled ham- about 6 eggs-1 heaping teaspoon grated Parmesan cheese for each egg-salt & pepper-chopped parsley
Beat eggs-add cheese–salt-pepper & parsley. Make thin omelets **(just until set)** and cover meat mixture-Put slices of ham on omelets and roll jelly – roll fashion. Bake uncovered 350 degrees-40 to 45 min. until done.

She didn't say how big to roll...just blanks...she placed it in a cookie sheet and roll to the width but not to the length... less than ½" thick...I think ...if my memory serves me right...2 # of meatball mixture filled a whole cookie sheet

In the margin: Mary Lazzuri filling...1 slice of mortadella- 1 slice proscuitto-hard boiled eggs-mozzarella

Italian Sausage

10 oz salt-50 # ground meat

5 # gr. pork-4 tsp salt-a good pinch of fennel seed per pound of meat.-about 1 tsp red pepper per pound of meat

In the margin: 3 scant tsp salt...later changed to ...½ tsp per # meat...I don't know how that translates to the 50 # of meat...someone do the math...when I make mine I use ½ tsp per pound...never made 50 pounds though

Italian Sausage...Frugal Gourmet

2 # pork meat (not too fat)-1 Tbsp gr. fennel-1 Tbsp dried parsley-3 cloves garlic crushed-2 Tbsps salt-⅛ hot pepper flakes (more if desired) ½ Tbsp fresh ground black pepper-4 Tbsps water-Mix thoroughly-stuff casings or make patties

Holiday Sausage

To Italian sweet sausage add chopped parsley – grated Romano cheese **(wine?)**

Homemade Sausage Patties
(American breakfast sausage)

½ tsp pepper-2 tsps salt-2 tsps brown sugar-½ tsp sage-1 tsp marjoram-¼ tsp thyme-1 tsp parsley-2 # gr. pork

Mix seasonings, sugar & herbs together in mortar before adding to meat. Work into pork thoroughly

Swedish Meatballs (David Wade TV cook)

Melt 2 Tbsps butter in a skillet. Sauté ¼ to ½ cup finely chopped onions-a few minutes, briskly. Turn heat off
Place 1 egg in a bowl-beat briskly with a slotted spoon. Add ½ c fresh bread crumb-(finely pulverized) ½ c milk. Let stand a few minutes **(4 or 5)**. Add butter & onion mixture **[Leave residual in pan for flavoring sauce]** Add meat-¼ lb pork ground and 1 # ground chuck-add1 Tbsp sugar and ½ tsp salt-¼ tsp allspice-¼ tsp nutmeg-work into mixture. Shake in black pepper-Mix thoroughly.
Add 2 Tbsps butter into skillet with residual. Make small meatballs about ¾" in diameter. Recipe makes about 30 to 35 meatballs. Brown in hot butter in skillet **(Try rolling them around in frying pan instead of turning with a spoon-to brown the other side)** Let butter remain in skillet. Meatballs go into a hot casserole-Add-¼ c flour-brown a very little **(not too dark)**, pour in 1 c water when it thickens-add ___cup ½ & ½ light cream-black pepper-1 tsp sugar-½ tsp salt. Cook a little while then add meat balls to sauce and heat through. **Good over noodles**

In the margins...get this...Lucy's birthday I used 1 # pork, 2 # beef, 3 Tbsps dried onion, 1 Tbsp sugar, ¼ tsp allspice, ½ tsp nutmeg, 1 tsp salt

Also in margin...some dried parsley, 1 tsp Worcestshire sauce, next to ¼ tsp allspice she wrote ..."a little less"...next to sugar she wrote ½ Tbsp...and "gravy in Betty Crocker's Cookbook"...there was no amount for the half and half... wing it!!

CAKES

Josie's sister Mary in her early 20's

Chocolate Oil Cake

3 c flour sifted
2 c sugar
1 tsp salt
make a well and add
1 or 2 eggs
2 c milk
2 tsp vanilla
2 tsp baking soda
mix together 1 c cocoa and 1 c oil- add to well-bake 35 min @ 350 degrees

my all time favorite...I had to ask Lucy to find this as it was not in her cookbook...she got it from Barbara who found it in Aunt Mary's stash...Josie made this all the time when we were growing up...makes fabulous cupcakes...she made them daily and Daddy would sell them at the gas station... may bake in bundt or 13x9...whatever you prefer

Tommy Toe Cake (Aunt Angie)

8 Tbsps oleo melted
2 cups sugar
2 eggs
½ cup sour milk
6 Tbsps cocoa
2 cups flour
2 tsp baking soda
2 scant tsp salt
2 tsp vanilla
1 cup boiling water

Melt oleo, add sugar, unbeaten eggs and milk. Sift cocoa, flour, salt and soda. Add vanilla-lastly boiling water. Mixture will be very watery. Start to bake at 350 degree oven 40 min

Josie's Recipe Collection:

Icing

1 cup granulated sugar
2 Tbsps cocoa
2 Tbsps corn starch
½ tsp salt
1½ cup boiling water

Mix sugar, cornstarch and cocoa, add water. Stir until smooth. Cook in saucepan stirring constantly. When thick remove from heat and add butter ...size of egg...add tsp vanilla and cup of chopped walnuts...pour on cake when cool...pour onto cooled cake.
Got this from Lucy...another all time favorite...mom loved it after I told her about the pudding like topping...my cousin Geri and I once ate the whole bowl of topping on my aunt while she was waiting for the cake to cool

Sunshine Cake (Alta Comes)

1 pkg batter recipe cake mix-1 11oz can mandarin oranges & juice-4 eggs-½ c oil
Mix oil-oranges & juice-add eggs-then add cake mix-Bake in 3 layers 350 degree oven 25-30 min. Do not overbake
Frosting-1-15 oz can crushed pineapple & juice-1 sm. box instant vanilla pudding-1 13 oz (or 12 oz) carton cool whip.
Mix pineapple and pudding mix-Fold in cool whip. Keep cake in refrigerator.

Lucy Shorer's Cake (Ronnie's Grandmother)

1 c flour-1 c sugar-2 heaping tsps b. powder-about ½ tsp salt Sift dry ingredients 3 times. Heat up 1 cup of milk to lukewarm-add to flour mixture. Beat 2 egg whites and add to mixture. Bake in bread pans in 350 degree oven for_____.

Quote Lucy Shorer "This makes the lightest cake ever"...this Lucy was the mother of my youngest brother's best buddy... And you're on your own with the baking time...I typed it as she wrote it...a blank space followed by a period.

Chocaroon Cake

(Mmmm tastes like a coconut choc candy bar)

2 egg whites-⅓ c sugar-2 Tbsps flour-1¾ c flake coconut-1 pkg choc cake mix-1 pkg choc pudding (inst)-2 egg yolks-1¼ c water-⅓ c oil

Beat egg whites until foamy. Gradually add sugar and beat until mixture forms stiff shiny peaks. Blend in flour & coconut-set aside. Combine remaining ingredients in lge bowl. Blend-then beat at med speed for 2 minutes. Pour ⅓ of batter into greased & floured 10" Bundt pan. Spoon in coconut mixture & top with remaining batter. Bake at 350 degrees-50-55 min. or until toothpick inserted in center comes out clean. Cool in pan about 15 min. Remove form pan & finish cooling on rack. Top with glaze.

Glaze-Add about 1 Tbsp milk to 1 cup xxxx sugar in a bowl-makes ⅓ cup.

Josie's Recipe Collection:

Banana Cupcakes (Bernetta Shoila)

½ c butter-2 eggs separated-1½ c sugar-2 c flour-1 tsp b. powder-1 tsp b. soda-1 c mashed bananas-½ c buttermilk ½ c walnuts-1 tsp vanilla-
Beat egg whites-add to batter
Bake 350 degrees-   minutes   makes   cup cakes

there ya go... those blanks again...how long to bake and how many the recipes yields try it and found out...and who is Bernetta?

Chocolate Cake

3 cups sifted flour-2 cups sugar-1 cup cocoa-1 tsp salt-2 tsps soda-2 eggs-2 cups water, milk or coffee-2 tsps vanilla-1 cup oil
Sift together-flour-sugar-cocoa-salt & soda-make a well-add eggs and 1 cup water & vanilla and oil-beat thoroughly add remaining water-Blend
Bake in 13x9x2" pan greased & floured-350 degrees-about 50 min

This may be the chocolate oil cake ...it is similar to the one Barbara found in Aunt Mary's file

Coffee Flavored Cake

3 eggs-½ c sugar-1½ c cake flour-1½ tsp b. powder-½ tsp salt-½ cup hot coffee-¼ c milk-2 Tbsps shortening-1 tsp vanilla
Beat eggs until very light. Add sugar, beating slowly constantly. Sift flour before measuring-resift with b. powder & salt. Stir into egg mixture. Combine coffee-milk & shortening and heat to boiling point. Add to batter and beat until well blended. Add vanilla-Bake in two lightly greased layer pans in a 350 degree oven for ½ hr. Ice with sea foam frosting-Sprinkle with almonds which have been cut into strips and toasted.

Aunt Mary's Sponge Cake

8 eggs-8 Tbsps flour-8 Tbsps sugar-lemon extract-Beat egg yolks-sugar & extract together. Beat whites and add yolks & sugar mixture and continue beating-add flour-Bake in greased and floured pans

I guess she forgot to mention to separate the eggs first... anyone want to guess what type of pan would bake this up the best.

Tiara Cake

Heat oven to 325 degrees-grease an 11" Tiara Dessert pan with shortening (do not flour)
2½ cups of yellow or white cake mix-combine cake mix 2 eggs-¼ c oil-½ cup water
Blend at low speed until moistened-Mix at med speed for 2 min.-Pour into pan & bake for 24-29 min.-Cake is done when toothpick comes out clean-cool cake on rack 5-10 min. Remove from pan by inverting bake onto cooling rack. Cool completely & place on serving platter. Store dessert in refrig-covered.

She writes: I take out enuf of the above & fill a small loaf pan-about a cup or 1½ c-the above is a little too much-causing it to go over.
I haven't a clue what a Tiara pan is...one of those large fluted tart things? In the margin she writes by the oil...Crisco, Wesson, Puritan...note the time is not 25-30 but 24-29

Mary Lazzuri's Jelly Roll Cake
Or Ice Cream Roll

1 c flour-1 c sugar-4 eggs separated-1 tsp baking powder-1 tsp lemon or vanilla-4 Tbsps water
Mix all but whites-beat well. Beat whites until stiff. Fold whites into batter. Put wax paper in pan-pour batter-smooth even-350 degrees about 20 min
Place on dish towel-sprinkle with xxxx sugar. Roll up-after 2 to 3 min-unroll and place ice cream on roll-Reroll-freeze overnight

I believe this is baked in a pizza pan

Stripe It Rich Cake

1 pkg cake mix (any flavor)
2 pkgs (4 serving size) Instant Jello Pudding (any flavor)
4 cups <u>cold</u> milk
1 cup xxxx sugar

1.)   Prepare cake mix as directed on pkg-baking in 13"x9" pan. Remove from oven. Poke holes at once down thru the cake into the pan with the round handle of a wooden spoon. Holes should be one inch apart

2.)   Only after poking holes-combine pudding mix with sugar in large bowl. Gradually stir in milk. Then beat at low speed of electric mixer for not more than one minute. (Do not over beat). *Quickly before pudding thickens* pour ½ of the thin pudding evenly over warm cake and into the holes to make stripes

3.)   Allow remaining pudding to thicken slightly then spoon over the top, swirling it to "frost" the cake. Chill at least one hour. Store cake in refrigerator.

CAKES

Dump Cake (Aunt Julia's)

1 pkg cake mix-1 stick oleo-1 can fruit. Pour fruit in cake pan. Sprinkle with the cake mix. Cut up oleo into small pieces over mixture. Bake 350 degrees about 45 min.

Short and sweet from the unkitchen Aunt. This is so Aunt Julia!

Banana Pudding Cake

1 or 2 small ripe banans-1 pkg yellow cake mix-1 pkg vanilla or banana instant pudding-4 eggs-1 c water-1¼ c oil-½ c nuts. Mash bananas add to remaining ingredients. Beat 2 min. bake 350 degrees 60-70 min. Cool in pan 15 min. remove from pan-finish cooling on rack. Pans should be well greased & floured. (13x9x2 350 degrees 50-55 min)

I'm guessing the first baking is a Bundt pan because of the length of the baking time

Mississippi Mud Cake & Frosting

Cake
1 c oleo-⅓ c cocoa-2 c sugar-1½ c flour-1 tsp. B. powder-4 eggs-1 can (3½ oz) coconut-1 c nuts (chopped)
2½ to 3½ c miniature marshmallows

Frosting
½ c softened oleo-½ c xxxx sugar-⅓ c cocoa-¼ c milk-1 tsp vanilla

Preheat oven 350 degrees-Grease 13x9 pan. In saucepan melt oleo-Add remaining ingredients & mix until blended. Pour into pan. Bake 40-50 min.

She notes: Prepare frosting while cake is baking

Dream Cake

1 pkg yellow-white or devils food cake mix-4 eggs- 1 c cold tap water-1 envelope Dream Whip Topping
Combine all ingredients in lge mixing bowl-Blend until moistened. Beat at med. Speed for 4 min. Pour into greased floured 10" tube pan-bake at 350 degrees 45-50 min. Cool tube cake for 15 min **(the other sizes 10 min)**. Then remove from pan & finish cooling on cake rack. Frost or sprinkle with xxxx sugar or top with fruit syrup or ice cream

Dream Cake can be baked in other size pans as well.
3 - 8" layer pans-35 min; 1- 13x9x2 pan 40-45 min; 2 - 9 " layer pans 30 min; cupcake pans about 20 min

Carrot Cake

(Antoinette's corrected by Doris Shedd)

3 c flour-2 c sugar-4 tsps b. powder-1 tsp b. soda-½ tsp salt-2 tsps cinnamon
Sift together-make a well and add 1 cup oil-4 eggs beaten-2 c grated carrots and 1 cup nuts. Bake –350 degrees 1 hr- Tube pan or 1 13x9x2 pan
Corrected...anybody know who Doris is?

Neopolitan Cake

1 pkg white cake mix-8 oz cream cheese-¾ c milk-4 eggs-1 tsp vanilla-¾ cup choc Quick-¾ c strawberry Quick
Blend together cake mix-milk-eggs & cream cheese. Divide into 3 equal parts. Into ⅓ of mixture add choc Quick-the 2nd third add strawberry Quick-to the last ⅓ add vanilla. Grease & flour tube pan-first add berry mixture-then vanilla-the choc batter last. Run knife thru batter-Bake –350 degrees 45-55 min.

Pistachio Sour Cream cake

1 pkg (18½ oz) cake mix (yellow)-4 eggs-½ c water-1 pkg instant Pistachio pudding-1 cup sour cream
Combine cake mix-pudding mix-sour cream and water. Blend to moisten-beat
2 min at med. speed. Pour into well greased & floured 10" Bundt pan or tube pan. Bake at 350 degrees 40 – 45 min. Remove from pan-cool on wire rack-Sprinkle with xxxx sugar

Sponge Cake (Mary Carboni's)

Beat 6 egg yolks until thick & lemon colored. Add ½ c cold water and continue beating until thick. Beat in 1½ c sugar gradually with ½ tsp vanilla, lemon, orange or lemon flavoring. Beat 6 egg whites until foamy. Add ¾ tsp cream of tartar. Beat until it forms stiff peaks. Fold egg whites into egg yolk mixture. Bake in 10" tube pan 350 degrees 1 hour. Cool in pan about 1 hour.

Pistachio Pudding Cake (Mrs. Dan Fusco)

1 pkg Duncan Hines white cake mix-2 pkgs Instant Pistachio pudding-½ cup oil-½ c milk-½ c water-5 eggs
Blend cake mix & pudding. Add oil-milk & water. Add eggs one at a time-beating well after each addition. Pour into greased 10 " tube pan. Bake 350 degrees for 1 hour.

Frosting

½ pt heavy cream-1 cool whip carton (4½ oz)-1 pkg Instant Pistachio pudding-Beat cream until thick-blend in Cool Whip & pudding

Josie's Recipe Collection:

Fresh Apple Cake

2 med apples-1 c sugar-1½ c flour-1 tsp b. soda-½ tsp salt-1 tsp cinnamon-½ tsp nutmeg-1 egg-1 tsp allspice-½ c shortening-1 c raisins-½ c nuts

Peel and core apples-Coarsely chop and measure 1¾ c in lge bowl. Add sugar-let stand 10 min. Sift flour- measure & add soda, salt & spices-sift again. Blend shortening & egg into apple mixture. Add flour mixture stirring-just until blended. Fold in raisins & nuts. Pour into greased 8" pan 350 50-55 min. Cool thoroughly. Sprinkle with xxxx sugar

She notes: Mrs Sanders' Fresh Apple cake...same as above only it called for melted shortening
My suggestion if you don't follow Mrs. Sanders' recipe it would be best to beat eggs and shortening and then add to apple mixture...otherwise your apples will be apple sauce
Mrs. Sanders was the cook at the school cafeteria.

Strawberry Cake

1 pkg cake mix-1 pkg strawberry jello-4 eggs-⅔ c oil-⅓ c water-about ½ qt sliced strawberries

Beat everything but berries for 4 min. Fold in berries. Bake 350 degrees 40 min 9x13x2 pan

She notes: I had just a few frozen berries-thawed them drained the juice and used it as part of water

Strawberry Cake

1 box white cake mix-1 pkg strawberry jello-1 c oil-½ c milk-
4 eggs-1 c nuts-1 c frozen strawberries-1 c coconut. Mix & sift
cake mix & jello. Add other ingredients in order given. Bake in
3 layers 350 degrees. Bundt pan 50 55 min **(check at 40 min)**

Filling
Cream together–1 stick oleo-1 box xxxx sugar-add ½ c drained
strawberries-½ c cocnut-½ c nuts-If too thick add a few drops
of strawberry juice
**Bake in 3 layers...does that mean it makes 3 - 8" rounds...
and for how long should we bake..30 min I guess.**

Swedish Coffee cake

½ c butter or oleo-¾ c sugar-2 eggs unbeaten-1 c sour cream-
1tsp. b. powder-1 tsp. b. soda-¼ tsp salt-1 tsp vanilla-2 cups
flour (a little less if dry)

Nut mixture: ½ c nuts-¼ c sugar-1 tsp cinnamon

Cream butter & sugar-add eggs to creamed mixture-Add
vanilla-sour cream & sifted dry ingredients. Put less than
half of the batter in greased 10" tube pan and sprinkle with
½ of the nut mixture. Pour rest of batter in pan-sprinkle with
remaining nut mixture. Bake 350 degree oven 40-50 min
Chopped dates & nuts may be used for filling

Cream Cheesecake (Karen's)

1 8 oz pkg cream cheese-1 c oleo-1½ c sugar-1½ tsps vanilla-
8 oz jar maraschino cherries (chopped & well drained) ½ c
nuts-4 eggs-2¼ c cake flour-1½ tsp b. powder
Combine sugar-cheese-oleo & vanilla-blend well-add eggs-
1 at a time-Mix well-gradually add 2 c flour sifted with
b. powder-Toss remaining flour with cherries & nuts. Fold
into batter. Cool 5 min. Remove from pan. Cool

3 greased & floured 1 # coffee cans-⅔ full-325 degrees-1 hr
4 greased & floured 1 # shortening cans-⅔ full-325 degrees-1 hr
5 greased & floured 5¾ x 3½ " loaf pans-⅔ full-325 degrees-
45-50 min
5 greased & floured 4 x 7 x 2" loaf pans-⅔ full-325 degrees - 50 min
5 greased & floured 3 x 5 x 1½-loaf pans-⅔ full-325 degrees-
35-40 min

Drizzle with glaze-1½ c xxxx sugar-2 Tbsps milk-Garnish
with cherries and nuts-Make ahead for Christmas gifts-wrap
securely-freeze-Thaw wrapped at room temperature

Raisin Bars (B.H. & Garden)

Combine 1 cup dark or light seedless raisins and 1 cup water-bring to boiling pt.-remove from heat and add ½ cup oil-Cool to lukewarm. Stir in 1 cup sugar and 1 slightly beaten egg. Sift together-1¾ c sifted flour-¼ tsp salt-1 tsp b. soda-1 tsp cinnamon-1 tsp nutmeg-1 tsp allspice-½ tsp cloves. Beat into raisin mixture-Stir in ½ c chopped nuts. Pour into greased 9x13x2 " pan. Bake in 375 degree oven 20 min or until done. Dust with xxxx sugar or drizzle thin white icing over it.

She makes this note: 40 cents sans nutmeats....and each square was certainly worth 40 cents...and how many of these did we eat!!!...these were a weekly treat as I recall

Upside Down Shell Cake (Pan)

Melt in Upside Downaire Pan-5 Tbsps butter. Stir in until dissolved ½ c brown sugar (firmly packed). Sift together 2 c flour-2½ tsp b. powder-½ tsp salt-¾ c brown sugar. Combine 2 eggs well beaten-¾ c milk-¾ tsp vanilla. Add flour mixture gradually until well blended. Stir in ½ c melted shortening (less 1 Tbsp). Beat until creamy. Pour batter into pan-Bake 350 degrees-1 hr. Loosen cake from sides and bottom of pan with spatula & turn on plate. Serve plain or decorate with strawberries & whipped cream. This pan may be used for shell cakes-baked Alaska or gelatin mold

I know I don't have an upside downaire pan in my cupboard...I never knew Mom to have one either

Josie's Recipe Collection:

Rum Cake

1 c chopped nuts-4 eggs-½ c cold water-½ c oiol-1 pkg yellow cake mix- 1 pkg inst vanilla pudding-½ c Bacardi dark rum
Glaze: ¼ lb. butter-¼ c water- 1 c granulated sugar
Preheat oven to 325 degrees-Grease & flour 10" tube pan or 12 c Bundt pan. Sprinkle nuts over bottom of pan. Mix cake ingredients. Pour batter over nuts. Bake 1 hr. Cool. Invert on plate. Prick top-drizzle glaze evenly over top & sides. Allow cake to absorb glaze. Use all of glaze.
To make glaze-melt butter in saucepan. Stir in water & sugar-boil 5 min. Stirring constantly. Remove from heat-stir in rum. Optional-decorate with whole maraschino cherries and border of frosting or whipped cream.

She has a question mark after ¼ lb butter in glaze (?)...does this mean more or less.

Pina Colada Cake

⅓ c rum-1 small inst. Coconut cream pudding-4 eggs-½ c water-1 box yellow cake mix-¼ c oil
Mix above ingredients well. Pour into 2 layer pans or tube pan. Bake 350 degrees 25-30 min
Icing for above
1 9 oz Cool Whip thawed-1 8 oz can crushed pineapple with juice

I guess you mix together and top

Cranberry Pound Cake

1 pkg yellow cake mix-1 carton (8 oz) plain yogurt or sour cream-4 eggs-1 c chopped frozen cranberries-½ c nuts
In lge bowl-combine dry cake mix-yogurt & eggs. Blend at low speed until moistened. Beat 2 min. at med. speed. Scraping bowl occasionally. Fold in cranberries & nuts. Pour batter into generously greased & lightly floured 10" Bundt pan. Cool completely. Warm ½ c Vanilla Ready to Spread Frosting and glaze cake if desired.

Depression Cake

2 c sugar-2 c strong coffee-water-or apple juice-½ c shortening-2 c dark raisins or diced pitted prunes.1 med. Size apple, peeled and shredded-2 cups un-sifted flour-1 tsp b. soda-2 tsps b. powder-1 tsp cinnamon-1 tsp cloves-1 tsp allspice-1 tsp nutmeg-1 c chopped nuts
In a med. Saucepan, simmer sugar-coffee and shortening-raisins & apple together for 10 min. Stirring occasionally. Cool 10 min. In lge bowl mix together flour-b. soda-b. powder-all the spices & nuts. Pour cooled sugar-raisin mixture into dry ingredients-Mix well. Pour batter into greased 13x9x2" pan-bake in 350 (?) degree oven for 25-30 min.-until center of cake springs back when lightly pressed with finger. Cut when cool-Cake keeps well.

She notes another question mark...does that mean 350 is too hot or too cold...

Josie's Recipe Collection:

Christmas Rainbow Cake

1 pkg white cake mix-1 pkg (3 g) Raspberry jello-1 pkg lime jello-2 c boiling water-1 container 9 oz Cool Whip thawed
Prepare cake mix as directed on pkg-baking in 2 well greased & floured 9" layer pans at 350 degrees 25-30 min. Cool in pan 15 min. Poke with fork at ½" intervals. Do not remove from pans. Dissolve each pkg jello separately in cup boiling water. Pour raspberry jello over 1 layer. Lime over the other. Chill 4 hrs. Un-mold 1 layer onto serving plate-top with 1 cup cool whip. Un-mold 2nd layer onto first. Frost top & sides with remaining Cool Whip. Chill-garnish with flattened gumdrops cut to resemble holly.

She has a picture in the margin: two green rectangular gum drops with a red circle ones adjacent to the 2 green gum drop leaves

Zucchini cake (Mary Carboni's)

Hand mix together-3 eggs-1 cup oil-2 tsp vanilla-2 cups grated zucchini- 2 c sugar
To the above add-3 cups flour-¼ tsp b. powder-2 tsps cinnamon & 1 tsp salt sifted together. Lastly add-1 can (lge) pineapple tid bits-1 cup walnuts-1 cup choc chips-2 sliced bananas. Grease pan very thickly & flour-Bake 1 hr-20 min-325 degrees

Sour Cream Pudding Cake

1 pkg cake mix-1 pkg inst pudding-1 c sour cream-⅓ c oil-4 eggs
Combine ingredients. Blend at low speed. Then beat 4 min at med. Speed. Pour into 2 loaf pans which have been lined on bottom with paper. Bake 350 degrees 45-50 min. Cool in pans 15 min before removing from pans

Fruit Cocktail Cake

2 c flour-1½ c sugar-2 tsps b. soda-¼ tsp salt-2 beaten eggs-
No. 2 can fruit cocktail & juice
Beat eggs until thick & lemon colored. Add fruit cocktail-then
add sifted dry ingredients (beat batter for full 4 min). Pour
into 2 greased & floured 9" cake pans. Sprinkle the top with
brown sugar-coconut & nuts. Bake at 375 degrees-45-60 min.
Glaze-Boil together ¾ c sugar-½ c evap milk and 1 stick oleo.
Boil for 1 full minute. Add 1 tsp vanilla & ½ c nuts. Pour over
hot cake. This cake is a sponge type cake-no shortening.

Fruit Cocktail Cake

Same as above except add ⅓ c evap milk-Bake in Bundt pan
at 350 degrees-30 min or until done. Cool 10 min-turn out on
serving tray & pour glaze on warm cake.

Fruit Cocktail Confetti Cake

1 pkg lemon cake mix-3 eggs-1 17 oz can Fruit Cocktail
Combine cake mix-undrained fruit & eggs in lge mixer bowl.
Beat as pkg directs. Turn batter into well greased & floured
tube pan. Bake at 350 degrees for 1 hr or until it tests done.
Cool 20 min. Remove from pan-Cool completely on wire rack.
Frost as desired.

Famous Lemon Cake (White House Cookbook)

¾ c butter or oleo-1¼ c sugar-8 egg yolks-2½ c cake flour-3 tsp b. powder-¼ tsp salt-¾ c milk-1 tsp vanilla-1 tsp lemon juice

Preheat oven to 325 degrees-Cream butter-sugar & 1 tsp lemon rind until light & fluffy. In a separate bowl beat egg yolks until light and lemon colored. Blend into creamed mixture. Sift together cake flour-b. powder & salt-resift 3 times. Add sifted ingredients in thirds-alternating with milk. Beat batter thoroughly after each addition-add vanilla-lemon rind & lemon juice. Beat 2 min. bake in well greased & floured Bundt pan for 1 hr or until done. Dust with xxxx sugar.

No mention of rind in list of ingredients...but apparently the recipe calls for it. She wanted a Zester so badly but couldn't find one...I had just bought her one from Pampered Chef... she never got to use it.

Apple Squares (Abie)

Dough-3 cups sifted flour-¾ tsps salt-1½ c oleo (3 sticks)-1egg+ 1 yolk-1½ Tbsps lemon juice-7½ Tbsps cold water-Mix as for pie crust
Filling-1½ c sugar-¾ tsp salt-3 Tbsps tapioca-1½ tsp cinnamon-¾ tsp nutmeg-1 can applesauce
Mix well together the filling ingredients. Cut the dough in half & roll out on a cookie sheet. Spread filling and cover with remaining dough. Bake until light golden brown. When cool dust with xxxx sugar & cut into squares. {375 degrees-30 min (?)}
Another question mark with cooking time...how much applesauce????

Cannoli Cake (Special Christmas treat)

3 eggs-1½ c sugar-1½ c flour-1½ tsps b. powder-¼ tsp salt-¾ c milk-1 Tbsp butter or oleo

Cake filling: ¾ c sugar-3 Tbsps cornstarch-¾ c milk-1 lb ricotta cheese-1½ tsps vanilla-½ c semi sweet choc chips (coarsely chopped)

Prepare cake:
Beat eggs until thick & lemon colored, with electric mixer-gradually beat in 1½ c sugar-beat 4 minutes-Stir together flour-b. powder & salt. Add to egg mixture-stir just until blended. Heat ¾ c milk & butter or oleo, just until butter melts-stir into batter.
Pour into 2 foil lined 9 x 1½" round baking pans. Bake at 350 degrees 25-30 min. Cool completely-remove from pan. Split layers in half to make 4 layers.

Prepare Filling:
Combine ¾ c sugar & cornstarch in a saucepan, slowly stir in ¾ c milk. Cook until thick & bubbly. Stir constantly-cover surface with wax paper-cool without stirring, with electric mixer beat ricotta until creamy, blend in cornstarch mixture & vanilla-Stir in choc chip pieces. Spread filling between layers. Frost with whipped cream.
Note: refrigerate cake

Josie's Recipe Collection:

Coconut Carrot Cake

2 c flour-1 c oil-2 c grated carrots-2½ tsps b. soda-2 c sugar-1⅓ c Angel Flake Coconut-2 Tsps cinnamon-3 eggs-½ c chopped nuts-1 tsps salt-1 8 oz can crushed pineapple in juice. Mix 1ˢᵗ 4 dry ingredients-Beat oil-sugar and eggs thoroughly-Add flour mixture-Beat until smooth-Add pineapple-carrots-coconut & nuts. Pour into greased 13x9x2" pan-Bake at 350 degrees-60 min. Cool 10 min-Remove from pan-cool on rack

Frosting: 1 cup Angel Flake Coconut-Cool – cream 1 3 oz pkg cream cheese with ¼ c butter. Alternately add 3 c xxxx sugar-1 Tbsp milk-½ tsp vanilla. Add ½ of the coconut. Frost cake-top with rest of coconut.

Yum Yum Cake (similar to Marie Lille's)

3 c flour-1 tsp b. powder-1 tsp b. soda-½ tsp salt-15 oz raisins-2 c sugar-1 c black coffee-2 Tbsps vegetable shortening-1 tsps cinnamon-½ tsp allspice
Preheat oven tp 350 degrees-butter and flour a 10 cup Bundt pan-Combine flour-b. soda-b. powder and salt. In large pot, over high heat, combine raisins-sugar-coffee-1 cup water-shortening-cinnamon cloves-nutmeg and allspice. Bring to a boil. Cook 5 min-Cool slightly-Stir in flour mixture until well combined-Pour batter into pan-Bake 50 min to 1 hour or until toothpick inserted into center comes out clean

This note in margin: Spice cake-old recipe-could be baked in pie pastry lined pan spread with raspberry jam-pour in batter-13 x 9 x 2"...check on baking times

The Famous Wesson Chiffon Cake

2 eggs, separated
1½ cups sugar
2¼ cups sifted cake flour
3 tsps b. powder
1 tsp salt
⅓ cupWesson oil
1 cup milk
1½ tsp vanilla

You make this famous cake with Wesson, the sparkling oil that inspired its creation. Heat oven to 350 degrees. Lightly oil and flour two 8 or 9 x 1½ " layer pans. In small bowl, beat egg whites until frothy. Gradually add ½ cup sugar, beating until egg whites are very stiff. Sift remaining sugar, flour, b. powder, and salt into another bowl. Add Wesson, half the milk, vanilla. Beat 1 minute. Add remaining milk, egg yolks. Beat vigorously 1 minute more. Fold in egg whites. Bake 30 to 35 minutes.

For orange filling: Blend 3 Tbsps cornstarch with ½ cup sugar; add 2 cups orange juice. Cook over medium heat until. Cool; fold in 1 cup orange sections, drained.

For Icing: Blend 2 cups sifted confectioners' sugar with 4 or 5 Tbsps milk and 1 tsp vanilla. Drizzle over top and sides of cake. Decorate with grated orange peel.

This recipe is copied directly from a Wesson advertisement. Josie made this cake so many times they are too numerous to count. She made a variety of toppings and fillings for so many occasions. She could make it from scratch without a recipe.

This is the last cake entry because my sister Lucy called me 24 hours before I was to turn the final copy into the publishers and said, "Stop the Presses! Stop the Presses!" She realized after looking through some old recipes that <u>THE</u> chiffon cake was missing from the cookbook. My mother used an angel food cake pan to bake a towering creation from this recipe.

Pineapple Squares (M. Lore)

4 c sifted flour-¼ tsp salt-1¼ c oleo-2 eggs beaten light-1 c sugar-2 tsps b. soda-¾ c sour cream

Mix dry ingredients & shortening as for pie dough. Add eggs and sour cream- mix thoroughly-Chill overnight. Roll half of dough to fit 16x12" cookie sheet-Place dough in pan-spread pineapple filling. Roll remaining dough to fit top. Brush with slightly beaten egg. Sprinkle with 1 cup nuts. Bake 30 min at 350 degrees-Cool-Cut in squares-Sprinkle with powdered sugar

Filling: 3 tsps cornstarch-1 cup sugar mixed with juice from can of crushed pineapple (No. 2½ can) Cook until thick add pineapple.

The following correction for the filling: 2   20 oz cans unsweetened pineapple-1¾ c sugar-6 Tbsps cornstarch

Cream Cheese Muffins

2 cups flour-2 sticks oleo (very soft)-½ # cream cheese-2 tsp vanilla-Roll into small shaped balls-work into muffin tins (small size)

Fill with the following: 1½ cups pecans-1 stick of oleo-2 eggs-¾ cup brown sugar-Bake at 375 degrees-15 min-Cool and dip in xxxx sugar

Her notes: ery lightly greased tins-try less oleo in filling-½ or less...after check ¼ cup

Beginners Doughnuts

(Drop variety) 2 doz balls
Sift together 1½ cups flour-2 tsps b. powder-¼ tsp salt-⅓ tsp nutmeg-½ c sugar-Combine 1 beaten egg-½ cup milk-¼ tsp vanilla-Mix lightly-Avoid over mixing-Drop by teaspoons in hot shortening (375 degrees)-Turn over at once-Leave until brown on underside-Keep frying temp 365 degrees-Turn to brown second side-When golden all over (about 4 min)-drain and dust with sugar

Rolled Doughnuts (1½ doz)

Sift together 1¼ cups flour-4 tsp. b. powder-¼ tsp slat-⅛ tsp nutmeg. Beat together 1 egg-½ c sugar-¼ tsp vanilla-1 Tbsp melted shortening-add ½ cup milk
Mix liquids lightly into dry ingredients-Chill dough for easy rolling. Roll out gently on lightly floured board to ¼ to ½ thick. Cut & fry in hot shortening (375 degrees). Turning when doughnuts rise and brown-turn- brown second-side-Drain.

Topping for Dough Nuts

No.1   Melt ½ cup semi sweet choc in double boiler-Dip top of 8 doughnuts in melted choc-Then in coarsely chopped walnuts

No.2   2 tsp instant coffee-2 Tbsps water-½ cup flaked coconut-1 cup sifted xxxx sugar-2 Tbsps cream or milk. In a pint jar dissolve coffee I water-add coconut-cover & shake until coconut is coffee colored. Spread coconut on ungreased cookie sheet-dry in slow oven 300 degrees for 25 min-stirring occasionally. Make icing-frost doughnut-while icing is soft sprinkle with coffee flavored coconut (enough for 12 doughnuts)

Josie's Recipe Collection:

****

Frosting

Butter Cream Frosting (Elinor Mabbett-Mrs. Foglia's)

1 cup milk-5 Tbsps flour-Boil to a thick paste-Cool to lukewarm-Then add ½ c oleo-½ c Spry-1 c granulated sugar-1 tsp salt and 1 tsp flavoring. Beat in electric mixer until thick & creamy-

<u>Chocolate Frosting</u>: add ½ c cocoa to basic recipe

Note: omit salt if using 1 cup butter or 1 cup oleo instead of Spry and oleo mix...the Foligia's lived next door to us on Second Ave in the late 50's

Someone asked me after reading this recipe "What is Spry?" It is another brand of vegetable shortening

Dream Whip Frosting

Into a deep narrow bottom bowl-pour contents of one envelope Dream Whip and 1 pkg (4 serving size) new improved Jello Instant pudding-any flavor-Slowly beat in 1½ cups cold milk to blend. Gradually increase mixing speed and beat until frosting forms soft thick creamy peaks (4-6 min) Makes 3½ cups frosting. For 4½ cups frosting-use a large (6 serving size) package Jello Instant Pudding and 2 cups cold milk

Hints

To make xxx sugar: take 1 cup granulated sugar and 1 Tbsp cornstarch-Put in blender & blend until powdery-Makes a scant 1½ cups.

To make condensed milk: Take 1 cup instant non fat milk-⅓ cup boiling water-3 Tbsps melted oleo-⅔ cup sugar-Pinch of salt. Combine all ingredients in an electric blender & process until smooth

Josie's Recipe Collection:

NOTES

DESSERTS

Aunt Julia in 1961 at 216 Fourth Ave on the upgraded
backporch

Grimaldi's Casata

Crust: 2½ c flour-½ c butter-½ tsp cinnamon-¾ c sugar-¾ c milk-1 Tbsp baking powder

Filling: 10 eggs-1 c sugar-4 # ricotta-juice of 1 lemon-4 ozs candied fruit-4 ozs chocolate chips-¼ c cherry juice

12" spring form pan
400 degree oven-lower rack-1 hour until firmly set

Grimaldi's was a great Italian restaurant on Bleeker Street in Utica, New York

Marie Sanita's Casata

Crust: 3 c flour-1 c Crisco-3 eggs-1 c sugar-3 pinches of salt-2 tsps of baking powder-¼ tsp cinnamon
Filling: 3 # ricotta-beat smooth-2 doz eggs, beat until foamy,-add 1¾ to 2 cups sugar gradually until thick and piles up softly. Stir ricotta & egg mixture together. Chop 1 small bottle maraschino cherries, drained, grated large Hershey bar and add to cheese and egg mixture-⅛ tsp cinnamon. Pat crust into pan-Fill-allow room on top for filling to raise

Note: next to the Hershey bar she had in parenthesis (39 cents)…does that mean the 39 cent size…try and find one now…no baking tips…have at it

Casata (no crust, Angie's)

3 # ricotta-1 # sugar-1 # walnuts-1 large sweet chocolate bar (melted)-1 doz eggs-1½ Tbsp vanilla
Beat eggs & sugar in bowl. Put ricotta in another bowl mix egg mixture a little at a time in the ricotta-Add chocolate and nuts. Bake in a 13 x 9 x 3" pan (do not grease) 1-1½ hours

Note: there were glops of batter all over this page...must have been a favorite of hers...there were no baking instructions...but for cooking in a large roasting pan this 3 # recipe...cook for 1 hour at 300 to 325 degrees...roasting pan... this I've never seen in her kitchen...baking a cheese cake in a roasting pan

**In the margin she notes that 1 cup of walnuts is plenty and that 7 oz of chocolate bar is the size...
Also to the side:
2 # ricotta-1⅓ c sugar-1 c nuts-8 eggs-1 tsp vanilla-chocolate bar about 5 oz must be a pared down version**

Chocolate Casata (Aunt Mary's)

1½ cups sugar-2# sieved ricotta-2 beaten eggs-2 tsps cinnamon-6 ozs melted chocolate-10 eggs beaten-
In margin-⅔ or ¾ c sugar...enough when using milk chocolate

Revised recipe squashed underneath this one: ⅔ or 1 cup of sugar-2 # sieved ricotta-8 eggs-2 tsps cinnamon-6 ozs melted chocolate or 1 cup melted chocolate chips...then crossed out 8 eggs and replaced with 10 eggs

Eggs are definitely 10 but you'll have to play with the sugar and the chocolate...no baking instructions

Josie's Recipe Collection:

Frances Izzo's Casata

2 # ricotta & 4 Tbsps milk beaten together-1½ cups sugar-2 tsps cinnamon-6 ozs sweet chocolate, grated-2 cans dried candied fruit peels-8 eggs, beaten

In the Margin: she writes...recipe baked in aluminum 9 x 12 at 325 degrees for 40 min. lower to 300 degrees for 25 min...
Where cans is noted I'm thinking they mean 2 of those little plastic rounds of candied fruit

Pineapple Casata (Angie's)

2 # ricotta-10 eggs-1 can No. 2 crushed pineapple-grated sweet chocolate-**sweeten to taste**
Cookie dough crust: 1¼ cups sifted flour-⅛ tsp salt-1 tsp baking powder-¼ c soft shortening-½ c sugar-1 egg-1 tsp vanilla-Mix ingredients to form a stiff dough-Chill-roll or pat into baking dish
She notes that ½ tsp cinnamon is optional in the dough recipe...sweeten to taste...what is that all about...add as much sugar as want

Then she writes: my version-1 # ricotta-1 No. 2 can crushed pineapple partially drained and sweeten to taste-10 eggs-1 large chocolate bar grated-fills glass baking dish-Bake 300 degree oven 1 hour-325 degrees ½ hour...cracks will appear in filling-check by inserting knife

Cinnamon Crisp Cheese Pie

Shell & topping: Combine 1½ c cinnamon crisp crumbs (1 packet) and 3 Tbsps melted oleo-Press into 8″ pie pan-Reserving ½ cup for topping
Filling: 2 eggs separated-½ c sugar-¼ tsp lemon rind-1 Tbsp lemon juice
Cinnamon crisp refers to graham crackers-1 packet of those

Beat 8 ozs cream cheese until fluffy - add egg yolks-sugar-lemon rind & juice. Fold stiffly beaten egg whites into cream cheese mixture. Turn into shell. Sprinkle with remaining crumbs. Bake in moderate oven (350 degrees) 25 minutes until slightly firm-chill 1 hr or more before serving

Nina's Cheesecake

4 c flour-2 tsps baking powder-½ tsp salt-4 oz butter or oleo-
2 eggs-4 ozs sugar **(½ c sugar)**-milk as needed to make smooth
dough **(4 - 5 Tbsps)**
mix like pie crust

Filling: 1½# cottage cheese-put through sieve. Make sure
cheese is dry **(drain off liquid)** 4 oz butter-6 eggs separated-
5 oz sugar-1 rounded Tbsp flour-1 level Tbsp cornstarch-1 tsp
baking powder-dash of salt-rind of lemon-1½ c sour cream-
white raisins or other canned fruit

Cream butter and sugar-add egg yolks-combine & sift together
flour-cornstarch, baking powder and salt. Add to creamed
mixture. Beat egg whites <u>and fold creamed mixture into the
egg whites</u>. Dot with butter before baking-350 degrees-45 to
50 minutes. Crust should be a nice golden brown.

**When adding fruit-if using raisins–first pour filling on crust-
then add raisins on top making sure they are covered
If using canned fruit-first drain fruit thoroughly and spread
over crust-then add filling**

**She has in parenthesis (more if needed)...this is squashed
in between the cornstarch and the sour cream and I don't
know which ingredient she was referring to...I am guessing
the sour cream because cornstarch was so specific**

Philly 15 minute Cheese Cake

*graham cracker crust

3-8 oz packages cream cheese-¾ c sugar-3 eggs- 1 tsp vanilla-
1 cup mini chocolate chips
Combine cream cheese & sugar mixing at med. Speed until
well blended. Add eggs, one at a time-mixing well after
each addition. Blend in chocolate pieces and vanilla. Pour
into crust-Bake at 450 degrees-10 minutes-Reduce heat to
250 degrees-continue baking 35 minutes. Loosen cake from
rim of pan-Cool before removing from pan. Chill.

Recipe calls for spring form pan 9"

Crust: 1 c graham cracker crumbs-3 Tbsps sugar-3 Tbsps
melted oleo

Cheese Cake (Mamie)

Bake 1 hr at 350 degrees (13 x 9 x 2")

1st Pineapple filling
1 package reg. vanilla pudding-1 # 2 can crushed pineapple-
Cook together until thick. Cool
**I am guessing here she means cooked pudding not instant
when she writes "reg."**

2nd cheese filling

2-8 oz packages cream cheese	1 Tbsp lemon juice
8 Tbsps sugar	3 cups milk
3 Tbsps flour	4 eggs

cream cheese with sugar & flour. Add eggs-2 at a time. Then add milk and juice. Beat well in mixture. Mixture will be watery

3rd crust

1½ sticks margarine	1 Tbsp baking powder
6 Tbsps sugar	1 egg
2½ c flour	

Mix butter, sugar-egg-flour and baking powder. Line in buttered pan-bottoms and sides-Pour cooled pineapple mixture over crust-than add cheese mixture. Bake as above

Cheesecake (Veronica Crystal)

2-8 oz pkgs cream cheese, softened
1½ Tbsps lemon juice

1½ c sugar
4 eggs, slightly beaten
3 Tbsps cornstarch

3 Tbsps flour
1 # creamed cottage cheese
1 tsp vanilla
½ c butter, melted
1 pint sour cream

Preheat oven to 325 degrees. Grease a 9" spring form pan

In large bowl beat (electric mixer) cream cheese with cottage cheese, eggs & sugar. At low speed beat in cornstarch, flour, lemon juice & vanilla. Add melted butter & sour cream. Beat just until smooth. Pour into greased pan. Bale 1 hr & 10 min, or until firm around the edges. Turn off oven. Let pan stand in oven 2 hrs. Then remove and cool 2 hrs. Then refrigerate 3 hours

Add Topping:
1 pkg frozen strawberries
drain berries, put juice in pan-add ¼ c sugar, about 2 Tbsp flour and red food coloring-cook and stir over low heat until thickened-cool-add berries

this page was pulled from a book...looks like a school cookbook of some kind

Cherry Casata

(my version-checked, very good)

1 # ricotta   ½ to ¾ c sugar
1 tsp vanilla   2 Tbsps cherry juice
5 beaten eggs
about ½ to ¾ c maraschino cherries cut in 3rds
about 3 or 4 oz shaved or grated sweet chocolate

Bake in 7 x 11" pan-300 degrees-45 min then 325 degrees 20-25 minutes

The following was noted just as "Filling"

Filling: 3½ cups ricotta-¼ cup flour-1 Tbsp orange peel-1 Tbsp lemon peel-1 Tbsp vanialla-½ tsp salt-1 tsp cinnamon-4 eggs-1 cup sugar-350 degrees about 1 hour

Danish Apple Pastries

2½ c flour-1 tsp salt-1 c shortening-1 egg yolk-1 c cornflakes-8 to 10 cups sliced apples-(about 4 pounds) ¾ to 1 cup sugar-1 tsp cinnamon-1 egg white
Combine flour & salt-cut in shortening-Beat egg yolk in measuring cup-add enough milk to make ⅔ c liquid. Mix & roll like pie crust. Roll ½ pastry 12 x 17-Sprinkle bottom of crust with cornflakes-top with apples-sugar & cinnamon. Roll other ½ of pastry & put over apples. Cut slits in top of crust. Beat egg white slightly-brush on top of crust.
Bake at 375 degrees for 50 min.
Glaze if desired: combine ½ c xxxx sugar-add a little milk & drizzle over pastry while warm

she notes... Very good pastry

Apple Crunch (Jane Nardi)

4 cups peeled sliced apples
½ cup water
1 tsp cinnamon
¾ cup flour
1 cup white or brown sugar
½ cup butter or oleo

Put apples in deep buttered baking dish-Add ½ cup water-In another bowl mix cinnamon, flour, sugar and butter with pastry blender. Spread over apples-Bake at 350 degrees-about 350 minutes

Serve warm with ice cream or whipped cream

Jane was our neighbor when we lived on Second Ave Extension...known as "The Reservation"...great neighborhood!

Mary Lazzuri's Pineapple Squares

2½ cups flour
¾ cup sugar
¾ cup oleo
Hand mix these until crumbly...**she notes "needs a lot more flour"**

Add: 2½ tsp baking soda-1 tsp vanilla-¼ cup milk-2 eggs-mix all ingredients to form a soft dough-divide into 2 balls-Refrigerate overnight before rolling

Rolling: use floured plastic wrap or between 2 sheets of wax paper-Makes enough for 1 large cookie sheet (14 x 10" pan)

Filling: 2 cans pineapple (20 oz each)-2 Tbsps cornstarch-2 Tbsps sugar-cook until juice from pineapple dries

Bake 350 degrees for 30 min.

She notes..."Needs about 3 more Tbsps corn starch & 2 more Tbsps sugar...filling is a little too much-I filled a large custard cup lined with dough"

Linzer Torte (Mary Lou Kreshe)

2 c sugar **(maybe ⅓ less)**-4 cups ground nuts (walnuts)-1½ c oleo-3 cups flour-2 Tbsps cocoa-1½ tsps cinnamon-1 egg-1 or 2 shots of whiskey
Cut shortening into dry ingredients until shortening is in fine particles-make a well and add whiskey & egg-Mix into a paste-form into a ball-chill about 2 hours-Roll out ⅔ of dough and cut to fit cookie sheet-Spread this with 18 oz raspberry jam-Roll out remaining dough – cut into strips about 1" wide/ ¼" thick-Make lattice topping-Brush with egg yolk & milk-Bake 350 degrees-50 to 60 minutes or until edges of strips recede from sides of pan. Cool-cut and wrap in foil-Store in cool place.

Strawberry Angel Food Dessert

(cost 1.35, 1.50 real cream)

1-3oz pkg strawberry jello-1-10 oz pkg sliced frozen strawberries*-1 Tbsp sugar-pinch of salt-½-10" Angel Food cake torn into pieces-½ pt whipping cream*

Dissolve gelatin in 1¼ cups boiling water-Stir in thawed strawberries-sugar-salt. Cool until it begins to thicken-Fold in the cream, whipped-Cover bottom of 9" pan with half the torn Angel Food-pour over half of the strawberry & cream mixture-make another layer of rest of the torn cake-pour over remaining strawberry cream mixture-Refrigerate 4 to 5 hours to set. Cut into tempting squares-garnish is optional

*fruit: or 1¼ cups of fruit including a little juice
*cream: 2 cups whipped, large Cool Whip container holds about 3½ cups

Sweet Ravioli (Caruso's recipe)

Filling: 2 # ricotta-sugar to taste-1 tsp cinnamon-2 eggs beaten-Mix all ingredients in large bowl- and set aside

Dough: 3 cups flour-2 eggs beaten-1 Tbsp oil-1 tsp salt-warm water

Place flour in a bowl-Make a well in center and drop in eggs, oil & salt-Add water a little at a time-just enough to make a stiff dough-Knead on a floured board until smooth-Cover & let set 5 minutes-Divide dough in half & roll on floured surface into 2 thin sheets-Drop teaspoonfuls of filling about 1½" apart on one sheet of dough-Cover with 2nd sheet-Press inverted 4 oz glass over each round and press firmly to cut through dough-Press around edges with fork-Deep fry in hot oil until golden brown-Drain on paper towels and sprinkle with xxxx sugar

Caruso's another great Italian café in Utica

Apple Strudel (Angie's)

4 cups sifted flour-1 cup sugar-2 tsps baking soda-1 cup shortening (oleo)-2 eggs-1 cup sour milk. Mix first 4 ingredients like pie dough. Add milk & 4 eggs **(very soft dough)**
Spread a little less than half of the batter in a greased 9 x 13 x 2" pan. Spread filling over this and add remaining batter on top of filling. **(Drop by teaspoons)** Bake @ 375 degrees for 50 minutes or until nicely browned. Drizzle glaze while warm or sprinkle with xxxx sugar
Filling: Cook 5 or 6 cups sliced apples in a little water about 10 minutes. Add 1 cup sugar-2 Tbsps flour-1 tsp cinnamon-Cook until thickened-Cook to lukewarm before using
Note: any canned fruit pie filling may be used-2 cans
½ of strudel fills a 9" square pan; if using 1cup sweet milk use 4 tsps baking powder instead of soda
who can forget the many many times we had this for dessert... in the same week!!!...especially during apple season

Fruit Cake (Mary Kinney)

3 c Brazil nuts-1 # dates-1 c cherries-¾ cup sugar-¾ c flour-3 eggs-½ tsp baking powder-pinch of salt-Mix all ingredients. Put in oven for 1 hr & 45 minutes at 325 degrees

Apple Crisp

21 ozs pie filling-1 tsp lemon juice-½ tsp cinnamon-¼ tsp nutmeg-6 Tbsps flour-¾ cups granulated sugar-3 Tbsps butter or oleo, softened-in 8" round cake pan place filling, juice, cinnamon and nutmeg. Stir to blend, set aside-In small bowl place flour, sugar & butter. With fork or fingertips-combine mixture until it resembles coarse crumbs-sprinkle over apple mixture. Bake 20 minutes @ 425 degrees or until crumb mixture is golden and apples are warm. Serve warm with softened vanilla ice cream. 4-6 servings

Josie's Recipe Collection:

Date Bars or Queen Elizabeth Cake

1 c chopped dates-1 c boiling water with 1 tsp baking soda dissolved in it-Pour water over dates-Let cool. Add 1 cup sugar-½ c shortening-1 egg-¼ tsp salt-½ tsp vanilla-1½ c flour sifted with ½ tsp baking powder-⅓ c nuts. Blend well and sprinkle granulated sugar over top. Bake at 350 degrees-45 minutes in 8 x 10 pan-needs no icing

Queen Elizabeth Cake

Same as date bars above except ¼ c shortening-⅓ tsp salt-1 tsp vanilla-1 tsp baking powder **(doubled in a 13 x 9 x 2" pan)** Bake 350 degrees in a greased and floured pan-single 35 minutes, doubled 45 minutes (?)

Icing for above- **(enough for 13 x 9 x 2" cake)** 3 Tbsps granulated sugar-3 Tbsps evaporated milk-3 Tbsps oleo. Boil 3 minutes & spread on warm cake. Sprinkle with coconut & nuts

sugar notes: in date bars recipe she has 7/8 c sugar squeezed next to the 1 cup; in the Queen E recipe she notes...try ¾ c sugar
the shortening in the Queen E recipe has "OK" next to the ¼ shortening...there you go play with the sugar content until it suits your taste

Mary Jane's Dessert

60 Ritz crackers-1 stick margarine softened to room temperature-2 Tbsps sugar-

2 pkgs pistachio instant pudding-1 qt ice cream-1½ c milk}**mix these together**

Put cracker crumbs on bottom of 9 x 13 x 2" pan-pour pudding over crumbs-sprinkle with more crumbs-top with cool whip-decorate with maraschino cherries

Note: she writes...put crackers in blender...mix oleo & sugar with crumbs

Rita's Chocolate Zucchini Cake

½ c soft oleo-1¾ c sugar-1 tsp vanilla-½ c vegetable oil-2 eggs-½ c sour milk-3 c un-sifted flour-½ tsp baking powder-4 Tbsps cocoa-1 tsp baking soda-½ tsp cinnamon-½ tsp cloves-2 cups grated zucchini-½ cup chocolate chips-½ cup nuts
cream oil, oleo & sugar-add eggs-vanilla & sour milk. Beat with mixer-sift together dry ingredients and add to creamed mixture. Beat well-stir in zucchini, chocolate chips-pour into greased & floured pan-sprinkle nuts on top
Bake: 9 x 13 x 2" pan @ 350 degrees 40-45 minutes
Bundt pan 50-60 minutes

Note: I put some of the nuts in the batter

Sponge Cake Dessert

Assemble cake in large mixing bowl (12 servings)

Make sponge cake in 2 layer pans
Make cream filling
Make custard sauce

Split layers to make 4 layers-sprinkle 4 layers evenly with rum-spread 3 layers with raspberry jam (3 Tbsps for each layer)-put layers together with cream filling (about 1 cup on each layer)-pour custard sauce over top-with whipped cream in pastry bag, decorate with rosettes on top of cake-insert toasted almonds over whipped cream-refrigerate several hours or overnight

Toast almonds on cookie sheet about 20 min until lightly brown

Custard Sauce: ½ c sugar-1 Tbsps corn starch-2 c milk-½ tsp grated lemon peel-2 egg yolks slightly beaten-¼ tsp vanilla-2 Tbsps light cream-In medium saucepan combine sugar and cornstarch-gradually add milk-stirring constantly-boil 1 minute-stir a little of the hot mixture into egg yolks-return this mixture to hot mixture in saucepan stirring-bring to boiling-remove from heat-refrigerate covered at least 3 hours stir in rum

Well this takes the cake...pardon the pun...had this all typed and realized the rest of the recipe was no where to be found...so there is no recipe for sponge cake or cream filling...no measure on the rum anywhere...any yellow sponge cake will do and some vanilla pudding filling...good luck here...there is a recipe for Aunt Mary's sponge cake in the cake section

Apricot Squares

⅔ c dried apricots	½ c flour
¼ tsp salt	½ c butter or ¼ c oleo &
	¼ c butter
¼ c granulated sugar	1 c brown sugar packed
½ tsp vanilla	1 c flour
½ tsp baking powder	½ cup chopped nuts

eggs (2?)

Rinse apricots-cover with water and boil 10-15 minutes. Drain-cool-chop. Mix until crumbly-butter-granulated sugar and 1 c flour. Pack this into pan-use greased 8 x 8 x 2" pan-Bake at 350 degrees about 25 min (20) or lightly browned
sift together ½ c flour-baking powder & salt-beat brown sugar into eggs-add flour mixture-mix well-stir in vanilla, apricots and nuts-spread over baked layer-return to oven and bake 20 minutes or until done-cool cut bars and roll in xxxx sugar

6 oz dried apricots = 1 cup

Orange Cottage Cheese Dessert

Mix a 12 oz carton cream cheese-1 can drained mandarin oranges-3 oz pkg low calorie orange gelatin-1 small can drained crushed pineapple-1 small bowl commercial type ready to spoon dessert topping-mix and refrigerate overnight

Pineapple Tortoni (Florence Henderson)

1 can crushed pineapple-1 banana-1 box vanilla instant pudding-½ c sour cream-maraschino cherries-flaked coconut
Drain crushed pineapple-Take 1 cup juice-put in bowl-add pineapple-add pudding-add sour cream-beat with beater-stir in mashed banana-throw in chopped nuts-cherries-add nuts & coconut-Fold in whipped cream or cool whip-Freeze

Josie's Recipe Collection:

Éclair Cake

2 small packages instant vanilla pudding-1 box graham crackers-3½ c milk-1 9oz Cool Whip (thawed)
Butter bottom of 13 x 9" pan-line with graham crackers-prepare puddings-beating until smooth-fold in cool whip-pour over crackers-make layers with pudding mixture and grahams-refrigerate 2 hours- then frost with Éclair Cake icing
Icing:
2 1oz pkg pre-melted chocolate-2 tsp lite corn syrup-2 tsp vanilla-3 Tbsps oleo, softened-1½ c xxxx sugar sifted-3 Tbsps milk-put all ingredients in bowl-beat until smooth-spread over cake & refrigerate for 24 hours

Coconut Apple Strips (very good)

2 cups sifted cake flour-1 tsp salt-⅓ c shortening-3 Tbsps water-3 Tbsps evaporated milk (undiluted)-4 c sliced tart cooking apples (about 4 med)-½ c sugar-½ tsp cinnamon-2 Tbsps oleo-1 egg, slightly beaten-½ c undiluted evaporated milk-½ c sugar-⅛ tsp salt-2 c flaked coconut-
Set out a 15½ x 10½" pan. Sift flour with 1 tsp salt into a bowl. Using pastry blender cut in shortening until mixture resembles cornmeal. Gradually add mixture of 3 Tbsps milk & 3 Tbsps water. Mix until blended. Turn dough onto a slightly floured surface and roll into a rectangle the size of the pan. Fit pastry into pan-arrange apple slices in rows on dough-overlapping slightly. Sprinkle evenly with a mixture of ½ c sugar & cinnamon. Dot with butter. Bake at 425 degrees-25 minutes. Remove pan from oven-reduce temperature to 375 degrees. Blend together beaten egg-½ c evaporated milk-½ c sugar-⅛ tsp salt & coconut. Spoon mixture evenly over apple slices. Bake 20 minutes longer or until top is golden brown. Cut into 2½ x 1½" strips. About 3 doz

Danish Pastry **(65 cents)** Mary Cross

2 cups flour-1 Tbsp sugar-¼ tsp salt-½ # oleo-2 or 3 egg yolks-1 pkg yeast-½ cup milk-2 egg whites-½ c sugar
Dissolve yeast in cold milk-add sugar-mix flour, salt & oleo as for pie crust-add egg yolks then yeast mixture-Put in refrigerator overnight. Next day take dough-divide in half-roll thin (13 x 16" rectangle). Beat egg whites stiff with sugar-Spread almond filling over dough-then spread with egg whites & sugar. Over this-sprinkle maraschino cherries-coconut-chopped nuts & raisins. Roll up like a jelly roll. Bake on lightly greased cookie sheet. 350 degree oven-30 minutes or until nicely browned. Drizzle glaze while warm-slice when cool

Note: for 2 rolls 1½ c coconut, 2 Tbsps cherry juice, ½ c quartered maraschino cherries, ½ c chopped walnuts, ½ c almond paste, 1¼ c raisins

In margin: Prune filling, nuts & coconut good also
Almond filling: ¼ c sugar, ¼ c chopped blanched almonds toasted, ¼ c oleo, cream sugar & shortening until lite and creamy, add nuts & mix thoroughly

Danish Puff (Mina's)

1 c flour-½ c butter-2 to 3 Tbsps water-mix as for pie crust-cut in two and make 2 strips on cookie sheet
Bring to a boil-1 c water-½ c oleo- add 1 c flour all at once, stirring-Add 3 to 4 eggs-one at a time, beating hard after each addition-add 1 tsp almond extract-spread the above mixture on the 2 strips-Bake at 350 degrees for 1 hour (until crisp)-Cool & frost with mixture of xxxx sugar, milk & almond extract. Top with chopped nuts

Josie's Recipe Collection:

Peach Kucken

Boiling water to peel peaches-2 # ripe peaches, peeled & sliced-2 Tbsps lemon juice

Batter: 1½ c sifted flour-½ c sugar-2 tsps baking powder-½ tsp salt-2 eggs-2 Tbsps milk-1½ Tbsps grated lemon peel-¼ c butter melted

Topping: ¼ c sugar-½ tsp cinnamon-1 egg yolk-3 Tbsps heavy cream

Pour boiling water over peaches-skin-place in large bowl-preheat oven to 400 degrees-sprinkle peaches with lemon juice-set aside

Sift flour, sugar, baking powder & salt in large mixing bowl. Using fork, beat eggs, milk & lemon peel. Add flour mixture and melted butter. Mix with fork until smooth, 1 minute. Do not over mix. Butter a spring form pan or a 9" round layer cake pan. Turn batter into pan. Spread evenly over bottom of pan.

At this point kucken can be refrigerated several hours

½ hour before baking combine sugar & cinnamon-mix well. Drain peach slices and arrange on batter around edge of pan-fill in center with 5 peach slices. Sprinkle evenly with sugar& cinnamon mixture. Bake 25 minutes-Remove from oven. With fork beat egg yolk and cream-Pour over peaches. Bake 10 minutes longer-Cool 10 minutes on wire rack-to serve remove sides **(plain layer cake pan serve from pan)**

*Serve with softened ice cream or cool whip

Chocolate Casata (Grandma Sgroi's)

⅔ cup sugar-2 lb ricotta-10 eggs (beaten)-1 cup melted chocolate chips-2 tsps cinnamon
¾ cup sugar-6 oz melted chocolate...use more sugar with melted chocolate and less sugar with the chocolate chips

Recipe baked in aluminum 9 x 12 pan-40 minutes at 325 degrees lower to 300 degrees-25 minutes

Crust for Casata (Grandma Sgroi's)

1¼ cups sifted flour-⅛ tsp salt-½ cup sugar-1 tsp baking powder-¼ cup soft shortening-1 egg-1 tsp cinnamon-1 tsp vanilla-½ tsp cinnamon (optional)-Mix ingredients to form a stiff sough-Roll or pat in baking dish

Casata (source unknown)

3½ cups ricotta-¼ cup flour-1Tbsp orange peel-1 Tbsp vanilla-1 Tbsp lemon peel-½ tsp salt-1 tsp cinnamon-4 eggs-1 cup sugar 350 degrees

a great more is unknown in this recipe...besides the author

Crust St. Anthony's Cookbook

Dough: Sift together 3 tsps baking powder-½ tsp salt-3½ cups flour-cream ½ cup shortening-1 cup sugar-Add 2 beaten eggs. To the creamed mixture add flour mixture alternating with ½ cup milk. Add 1 tsp vanilla. If sticky and hard to handle add more flour
If chilled-easier to roll or pat in pan

Josie's Recipe Collection:

Another Version of Pineapple Casata

1 # ricotta-5 beaten eggs-½ cup sugar if using sweet chocolate-½ chocolate bar (4 oz) grated-1 can No. 2 crushed pineapple-partially drained-7 x 11 baking dish

she adds this note under all her casata recipes "use your good judgment"...cracks will appear in filling as it bakes... check by inserting knife

Funnel Cakes

1¼ c flour-2 Tbsps sugar-1 tsp baking powder-¼ tsp slat-1 egg beaten-⅔ c milk-Blend first 4 ingredients-Beat egg & milk together. Add gradually to dry ingredients beating constantly until batter is smooth.

Holding finger over bottom of funnel (⅜ to ½" hole) fill funnel with batter. Hold funnel as near surface of heated fat as possible-remove finger and drop batter into 350-375 degree fat (fat 2" deep)

Using a circular movement from center outward to form a spiral cake-about 6" in diameter. Immediately replace finger on bottom of funnel-fill funnel and form other cakes-as many as will float un-crowded. Fry until cakes are puffy and golden brown-turning once. Remove with slotted spoon and drain over fat for a few seconds before removing to absorbent paper. Sift xxxx sugar lightly over cakes and serve them warm

Hold end of funnel close to surface of oil

Funnel Cakes (Better Homes and Garden)

2 beaten eggs   1 tsp baking powder
1½ cups milk   ½ tsp salt
2 cups sifted flour   2 cups cooking oil

Combine eggs & milk-add sifted dry ingredients to egg mixture-beat smooth with rotary beater-test to see if mixture flows easily through funnel

If too thick add milk, if too thin add flour

In 8" skillet heat oil to 360 degrees-pour a generous ½ cup batter into funnel-Fry until golden brown-about 3 minutes-turn with wide spatula & tongs-Cook 1 minute-drain on paper toweling-Sprinkle with xxxx sugar-serve hot
Makes 4 cakes...may serve with hot syrup

Funnel Cake

"I have made these" she writes

Mix 1 pint milk with 2 eggs, well beaten, 2 tsps baking powder, ⅛ tsp salt and about 3 cups flour-enough to give the batter the consistency of a thin waffle batter. It must be thin enough–though not as thin as pancake batter-to go through the easily. Have the deep fat ready and hot. Now pour from a pitcher, pour the batter through the funnel into the hot fat, which as deep as it would be for donuts.

Old directions say to begin at center of pan and turn the stream around in a gradually enlarging circle. We found it was much easier to do just the opposite-start at the outside and work in.
Fry to a light brown. Turn with 2 forks and fry on the other side until light brown. Drain on paper towels and serve hot with a sprinkling of xxxx sugar and tart jelly
Well there you have it …details at last…all the info for making funnel cakes…including 3 different ways to turn them

Rice Pudding (Mother Sgroi's)

1 qt scalded milk-1 cup boiled rice-½ c sugar-¼ tsp salt-2 eggs. Stir rice into milk-add sugar-salt-eggs slightly beaten-1 Tbsp butter may be added. Flavor as desired. Bake in buttered shallow dish till firm-
she notes: "Yolks only may be used-margarine instead of butter"…sorry no temperature

Lime Gelatin or Dessert (Edith Moran)

1 pkg lime jello-dissolve in 1 cup boiling water-then add 3 lge ice cubes and stir until dissolved. Drain 1 can crushed pineapple (small can) and add juice to gelatin. When it starts to set beat until frothy-then add the pineapple, small pkg (8 oz) cottage cheese-small container of cool whip & nuts chopped fine
"Best made one day ahead of serving"

Chocolate Ice Cream (Mother Sgroi's)

¾ cup sugar-2 Tbsps cocoa-1/16 tsp salt-⅓ cup hot water-1½ pints cream or evaporated milk (3 cups)-2 tsps vanilla
Mix sugar, cocoa & salt thoroughly-Add hot water-Heat until sugar is dissolved thoroughly-Continue cooking for approximately 5 minutes-Remove from heat and partially cool-Add cream & pour into freezing tray and allow to freeze firmly. Remove to chilled mixing bowl-add vanilla and whip with electric beater until mixture becomes light and creamy. Return quickly to freezing tray and allow to finish freezing

Pineapple Filling

Combine contents of 1 package (3¼ oz) of vanilla pudding-1 can (1 # 4oz) un-drained crushed pineapple-1 beaten egg-and 1 tsp lemon juice. Cook, stirring constantly until mixture boils and is very thick. Remove from heat. Cover with wax paper or saran wrap & chill. Whip 1 cup heavy cream until stiff. Gradually add ¼ c sugar. Carefully fold whipped cream into pudding mixture.
 May be used as cake filling

Ambrosia Salad (Mary Sylvester's)

1 cup miniature marshmallows
1 cup crushed pineapple (drained)
1 cup coconut
1 cup sour cream
1 cup any fruit...mandarin oranges, fruit cocktail (drained)
She notes: I use both

Refrigerate at least 6 hours, ½ cup nut meats-any kind Jello and Sour Cream (Mamie Oriole)

2 large pkgs strawberry jello
2 pkgs frozen strawberries
3 cups crushed pineapple
4 mashed bananas
1 pt sour cream
4 cups boiling water
Add water to Jello-then frozen berries and bananas. Place half of mixture in pan. Let it stand in refrigerator for about 10 minutes. The rest of the jello set aside at room temperature Spread sour cream over first half and pour the rest of the jello mixture over sour cream. Refrigerate

Cream Puff Filling

2 c milk
8 oz pkg cream cheese
vanilla instant pudding 3¾ oz pkg

gradually add ½ c milk to softened cream cheese and mix until well blended-Add pudding mix and remaining milk-beat slowly 1 minute-Cover surface with plastic wrap-Chill-Fill puffs-top with powdered sugar or Caramel topping

fills 8 cream puffs

Cream Puff Pastry (Betty Crocker)

Again she left us high and dry...filling recipe but no pastry recipe...my sister suggested just use Betty Crocker...also asked someone I work with who is a master baker...and she gave me much the same recipe

1 cup water-½ stick margarine or butter-1 cup all purpose flour-4 large eggs

Heat oven to 400 degrees-Heat water and margarine to a rolling boil in a 2½ qt saucepan-stir in flour-reduce heat to low-stir vigorously over low heat 1 minute or until mixture forms a ball-remove from heat
Beat in eggs, all at once, continue beating until smooth
Drop dough by scant ¼ cupfuls about 3" apart on un-greased cookie sheet
Bake 35 to 40 minutes or until puffed and golden
Cool away from draft
Cut off top one third of each puff-Fill with cream filling-replace top portion-add desired topping-refrigerate until served

Maple Walnut Cream Pudding (Julia's)

2 c milk-1 c maple syrup **(100% maple syrup)** 2 Tbsps corn starch-¼ tsp salt-2 eggs-½ c chopped walnuts-1 c cream (whipped)
Scald 1¾ c milk with the maple syrup in the top of a double boiler-Combine the remaining milk with the cornstarch and salt. Add gradually-stirring constantly-to the hot mixture. Cook 25 minutes-then add this mixture to eggs slightly beaten. Cook 5 minutes. Pour into serving dishes and sprinkle with chopped nuts while pudding is still hot. When cold cover with whipped cream

Cherry Jubilee Ice Cream

2 cups fresh dark sweet cherries-rinsed & stems & pits removed
1¼ cups sugar-2 eggs-1 tsp cornstarch-½ tsp vanilla extract-¼ tsp lemon extract-1 cup chilled heavy cream whipped

Finely chop or grind 1 cup of the cherries-quarter remaining cherries-set in refrigerator-Combine sugar & cornstarch in top of double boiler-mix well-Add milk & eggs-beat with rotary beater until smooth-set over boiling water and cook about 10 minutes-stirring constantly. Remove from heat and cool. Stir in the chopped cherries, extracts and food coloring a drop at a time until desired color is obtained. Pour into freezer trays and freeze until partially frozen-stirring occasionally. Using a chilled bowl and beater-beat mixture until smooth. Fold in the whipped cream & quartered cherries-return to trays-Freeze until firm stirring occasionally.

Hey hey...get out your rotary beaters...where is mine... when did I use it last!
I remember making ice cream with her when we lived on Palmer Street in the 1950's...she placed the ice cream in the metal ice cube trays to freeze...but I am sure kitchen specialty stores have something appropriate if you are so inclined to whip up a batch of ice cream...dark cherry ice cream was one of her favorites

No mention of food coloring in ingredients list...color me surprised!

Pumpkin Pie (mother Sgroi's) very good

3 cups pumpkin (or No. 2½ can)-2 cups brown sugar-1 tsp ginger-1 tsp salt-5 eggs-1 qt milk-6 tsp melted butter or oleo. Put in pie crust-Sprinkle with cinnamon (when done filling puffs up) and crackles-425 degrees 45-50 min. Insert silver knife 1" from edge of pan-if knife comes out clean-it's cooked-center may look soft but it sets as it cools.
Better cooked at 375 degrees for 50 min...boy she even edited her mother's recipes!!

One Thanksgiving I said to her "I think I'll leave the ginger out of the pumpkin pie this year and try it without." No! She raised her finger I had to put it in because Grandma Sgroi always used ginger...that's what made it...so I did...I was 40 something at the time!

Mincemeat Custard-very good

2 eggs-⅓ cup sugar-¼ tsp salt-1 cup milk-1 pkg mincemeat-single crust recipe pie pastry.
Beat eggs with sugar & salt. Add milk-Stir until thoroughly mixed-Line 9" pie pan with pastry. Spread prepared mincemeat (about 1½ cup) over bottom crust-Pour in custard mixture. Sprinkle with nutmeg. Bake in hot oven (425 degrees) for 15 min-reduce to 350 degrees-bake 25-30 minutes or until silver knife comes out clean. Decorate with wreath of cherries, citron and nuts.

Pie Crust (Mary Cerri's)

5 cups flour-2 cups shortening-1 egg in cup, fill with water to ¾ cup

Josie's Recipe Collection:

Pie Crust (Angie's)

5 cups flour-2 cups lard-¼ cup vinegar-water

ingredients only...that's all folks

Steamed Pumpkin

Preheat oven to 350 degrees-scrub pumpkin well. Cut in half or quarters or large chunks-to fit in Brown n Bag.
Half of one about the size of a basketball (10" dia) fits in a 14x20 Brown n Bag

Scrape out seed centers. Place pumpkin pieces in bag, cut side down. Place in 2" deep roasting pan. Close with twist tie-make 6 half inch slits on top. Cook until pumpkin pieces collapse. The basketball size cooks in 45-60 min. Cool-cut off corner of Brown n Bag, drape over corner of roasting pan and let all liquid drain out of bag. When pumpkin is cool enuf to handle, scrape "meat" from soft rind. If pumpkin still seems too moist-let stand in colander to drain to desired consistency. It may be sieved if a very fine texture is needed. A 10" pumpkin makes 6 to 8 cups of pumpkin puree

I place skinless raw pumpkin chunks in a large pot...no water...just a little salt...steam until soft...drain excess water and puree in blender...measure 1 cup servings and freeze... use in recipes that call for pumpkin...nothing like fresh pumpkin pie...noticeable difference in the taste...Libby's Pumpkin cookies with M & M's
Sooooooo good

Easy Apple Pie

Fill pie plate level with apples-Sprinkle with 1 tsp cinnamon-dash of nutmeg-½ c sugar-cover with aluminum foil-bake at 350 degrees for 20-25 min
Cake Batter: 1 Tbsp butter-½ c sugar-1 egg-1 tsp b. powder * heaping-1⅔ c flour-1 tsp vanilla-Spread over partially cooked apples-Bake 50 min in 375 degree oven uncovered

*heaping refers to flour or b. powder...she loses me with this note

Apple Pie (Keebler Crust) 8 servings

1 graham or vanilla crust-1 large egg yolk beaten slightly-5½ cups sliced cooking apples-1 Tbsp lemon juice-½ c sugar-¼ c lite br. Sugar packed-3 Tbsps flour-¼ tsp salt-½ tsp cinnamon-¼ tsp nutmeg-¾ c flour-¼ c sugar-¼ c lite br. sugar packed-⅓ c butter or oleo at room temp-omit lemon juice if apples are very tart

Preheat oven to 375 degrees-Brush bottom & sides of crust with egg yolk (evenly). Bake on baking sheet about 5 min or until lite brown. Remove crust from oven-combine apples-lemon juice-½ c sugar-¼ c br. sugar, flour, salt, cinnamon 7 nutmeg. Mix well-spoon into crust.
Mix remaining flour, sugar & butter with pastry blender until crumbly. Spread evenly over apples. Bake on baking sheet until topping is golden and bubbling-about 50 min. Cool on rack. Serve at room temp.

****

Josie's Recipe Collection:

NOTES

About the Author

Karen M. Talarico RN MSN

Karen grew up and lived in Central New York for 35 years. She currently lives in St. Augustine, FL where she raised her three children.

After the death of her mother Karen inherited her mother's recipe collection, which she edited to give to her family members. The project grew into this cookbook *Josie's Recipe Collection: From Cooks and Kitchens of Central New York.*

She has a background in critical care nursing, having been a nurse for 25 years. A graduate of MVCC in Utica, New York 1979 with an AAS in Nursing, she is practicing cardiovascular nursing at the present time. She holds a Masters Degree in Nursing.

Karen has been writing for a hobby for over 30 years. Her next project is to publish a children's book series and then her volumes of poetry. She has professional nursing articles that have been published.

Printed in the United States
21292LVS00004B/278